I must admit that my novel *Contessa* was well received even though the subject matter was not very well known when I wrote the book 20 years ago. I do hope you pass my book on to others to read.

You asked me how I came up with the theme of gender dysphoria for the book. It is very strange that in life large oak trees grow from a tiny acorn, meaning that just a kernel of an idea can result in something much larger.

I lived in Paris, France, during all of the seventies. I mainly taught school there, English as a foreign language. While there, I established The Paris English Theatre where nine of my plays were produced. That is actually where my writing career began. I returned to the states in 1980 because I was hired to write a screenplay.

Backing up a bit to the subject of transsexuals, during my time in France I tried to get back to Okolona at least once a year to visit my parents. On one such trip, I worked in a side visit to my brother Paul and his family in Louisiana. After a few days there, I was returning via New Orleans to New York where I would catch my charter flight back to Paris. I got to New York but our flight to Paris had been cancelled. The next available flight would be the next day. We were told that we could stay overnight in a hotel near the airport or go into the city. I chose going into Manhattan because that would be much more interesting than killing time near an airport.

After I checked into a downtown hotel, I went out for a walk. I passed a theatre that had a play called *Women Behind Bars* with Divine, a very popular drag queen. I had always thought Divine was a hoot so I bought a ticket to see the play that night. I thoroughly enjoyed the play. After it was over, I tried to get backstage to talk with either the producer or Divine and see if my Paris English Theatre could put on a production of it in Paris. Unfortunately, Divine had already split as well as anyone connected with the production of the play.

LETTER 1

JOY

Dear Joy,

Thank goodness for Facebook. What a surprise being in contact with you after seventy years. Sounds like we live in a time machine. I decided to reply by email rather than Facebook so I would have the luxury of being able to say more.

In your email, you stated that you had lived in San Francisco most of your adult life. I remember our first meeting when we began first grade together in Okolona. I must admit that I thought you were the prettiest and smartest person in class. I bragged so much on you to my mother that she accused me of having a girlfriend.

The truth is that you were smart and pretty. We remained friends but no boyfriend/girlfriend status – just good friends. However, in the tenth grade you decided to skip a grade by taking summer school classes. Thus, you graduated a year ahead of me. You were gone and I don't think I saw you again until your Facebook message the other day.

As I say, what a surprise to hear from you. I was so glad that you read my book *Contessa* and enjoyed it. You said you remember very well a lot of the experiences we shared together in that small town.

CONTENTS

PREFACE

*"My take on life is that it's a giant hors d'oeuvres tray and
my approach is to have a taste of everything." - Jack Fitzgerald*

Jack Fitzgerald is the author of several books and has produced many stage plays. He recently turned 89 and, in spite of failing eyesight, decided to write one last book. It had to be unique and different.

Fitzgerald's book consists of forty-two emails. They are replies to phone calls, greeting cards, and emails, none of which are in the book. What you do see though are forty-two email replies from Jack to these friends, relatives, and his readers. These emails build a matrix that in many ways is like a puzzle. From each email you will glean certain information about Jack's life. As you proceed through the book, you will get more and more droplets of information. By the time you finish email forty-two, you will have a rather complete autobiography of Jack's life. So, for once, you can have unusual fun reading someone's emails and clues to their life lessons and experiences. So, get started at once on this email puzzle and start collecting virtual autobiographical clues.

Best to you and have fun on your very first virtual autobiographical puzzle.

Cheers,
Jack Fitzgerald
Palm Springs, CA

Dedicated to:

Ken McCoy
Ron McCoy
Buzz Hagen
David Simonian
Dan Felix

MY VIRTUAL LIFE
AN ELECTRONIC AUTOBIOGRAPHICAL PUZZLE

iUniverse books may be ordered through booksellers or by contacting:

iUniverse
1663 Liberty Drive
Bloomington, IN 47403
www.iuniverse.com
844-349-9409

ISBN: 978-1-6632-3399-8 (sc)
ISBN: 978-1-6632-3398-1 (e)

Print information available on the last page.

iUniverse rev. date: 02/09/2022

MY VIRTUAL LIFE

An Electronic
Autobiographical
Puzzle

JACK FITZGERALD

Disappointed I returned to the hotel and settled for having had a very fun evening of theatre. The next day I was taken to the airport for the charter flight to Paris. During the flight my mind wandered back to the play I had seen the night before. I thought to myself that I wrote plays so why not write something with a drag character or some offbeat character. I don't know why but my mind turned to Christine Jorgensen who in the 1950s had changed sex from a man to a woman in Copenhagen, Denmark.

Suddenly my mind, like putting together certain ingredients to mix a cocktail, had the makings in my head of a new play, which I would call *Tijuana Lady*. By the time our plane landed in Paris I had the plot developed in my mind concerning a sex change, male to female, the character being a big porn star who had returned to her hometown, a small town much like Okolona, for the burial of her father. As imagined, all the small-town bigotry came gushing out and it was a very funny play.

I decided in Paris when producing *Tijuana Lady* that I should have a four-minute filmed trailer advertising a porn film called *Tijuana Lady*. After the showing of that trailer, the curtains then would open to a very ordinary home in a small Arkansas town. Then the fireworks would begin.

For help in producing the little film trailer, the entertainment critic for the *International Herald Tribune* introduced me to Wallace Potts, partner of the dancer Rudolph Nureyev, and his friend Oscar winning Spanish cinematographer Néstor Almendros. Together we made the filmed trailer.

The play opened with that trailer and then the audience witnessed three acts of fireworks on stage against small minds and narrow mindedness. The play was a very big success and was even optioned for a film by a British film company. (Unfortunately, the film did not get made.)

I was quite pleased that the play was doing so well. One night after a production, I was approached by a woman who worked for the United Nations Educational, Scientific and Cultural Organization (UNESCO) in the social management division. She asked me to come before UNESCO and give a lecture on gender dysphoria. I was caught between two worlds.

On one hand I actually knew very little about transgender people, but I had a fertile imagination. I really had no choice except to accept.

I worked very quickly at the American Library to check out anything I could find on the transgender subject. I did manage to find enough information, though sparse, to make it through the evening. It did make me seem like an expert which was definitely not the case.

Several years later I told all the above to my Aunt Elsie in Atlanta. She was quite elderly and not in very good health. She enjoyed my tale but told me that I should write it into a book. I did not think I would be able to do such a thing. I wrote plays but not books. She told me that if I didn't write it into a book, she would come back and haunt me. We had a good laugh and I returned back to my home in Palm Springs, California. But Elsie passed away about a year later. True to her word, I believe she did haunt me. I had weird dreams of her telling me I must write the book. So, one day having coffee at Starbuck's I thought that I might at least try to see if I could even begin writing a book. On a Starbuck's napkin, I wrote the preface to the book. That seemed to be all it took. I began writing the book and finished it after 800 pages. It published at 529 pages.

I only used certain plot items from the play *Tijuana Lady* in the book version which I called *Contessa*. In my book, I kept things very factual and did a ton of research. No longer was the transsexual main character a porn star but an actual show business personality who was very famous.

The book was published in the year 2000 and was very well accepted.

So, Joy, that is how a small-town guy from Okolona can end up writing about transsexuals while living in Paris, France.

My very best to you, and let's keep in touch.

Jack
Cheers, Jack

Main Street Okolona, MS.

LETTER 2

REBECCA

Dear Rebecca,

Thanks so much for your Christmas card with an abbreviated version of your yearly Christmas Newsletter. I realize that with all your family gone away from the nest and people passing on, such newsletters can shrink year by year. You mentioned having been in Okolona recently and, of course, the mention of that word starts the memory machine up.

I can remember oh so well when Ferman Jr., you and I were in high school. Ferman Jr. and I were two years ahead of you and were friends from about the age of five. I remember all the times I would come out to your family farm and spend the weekend and we would talk, talk, talk. I had nothing but a lot of ideas about how life was going to be for me when I left Okolona. To me it was a very small town and a microcosm of the outside world. I thought my life would be complete if I could ever make it to Hollywood or do something in the creative arts. You and Ferman Jr. listened patiently to all my dreams and seemed to share my aspirations.

I must say one thing about Okolona. During those years when I felt trapped in its small-town doings, Okolona seemed to be like a jail for me. I didn't realize though that without Okolona and that upbringing I could never have become a writer. When my brother Paul heard me express my desire to become a writer, he said that since I was a rather timid person I'd first have to live and get some experience in living.

What I didn't realize when my brother told me that I was that I was getting a great education in plot development. I have traveled all over the world and, yes, I have had many experiences which I have written about. However, I have written far more about Okolona. I didn't use actual names, but the situations were wonderful and made my writing popular. Most people said when they read something I had written that it sounded like me talking.

After I graduated from high school, I fled Okolona as quickly as I could. My first stop in this trip of mine through life was to go to Mississippi State University. It was a college in those days. That was exactly 37 miles from Okolona. However, it did get me away. Ferman Jr. and I went there together and were roommates.

Starkville, where Mississippi State is located, was not New York or Hollywood. However, it did not stop me from seeing if it couldn't be my New York.

Mississippi State was called Cow College because it was really an agricultural and mechanical learning center.

The world there centered around sports. Ferman Jr. and I had no such interest. We had to play like we were involved but it was a real act, believe me.

I noticed one thing at Mississippi State. It didn't have a theater group or anything similar. I had been in the junior and senior plays in high school. The casting was not first rate because we only had 21 students in my junior and senior class. Even though I was gladly in those two plays, which were directed by Miss Zaina Glass, an old maid. Miss Zaina directed the plays and did her best to make us look as good as she could. She was a very strict teacher, and I must admit she frightened me. I definitely was not one of her pets. She cast me in the plays though and I felt like I did very well given the circumstances.

With only being in those two plays as my background, I wrote a play at Mississippi State which I called *Good Grief.* I got to thinking that we should put it on. My brother, Paul, tried to interest me in a fraternity he belonged to. I didn't take to fraternity life. I was sure, with Ferman Jr.'s help that we could put on this play. So, I got the school newspaper, The Reflector, to sponsor the activity. Ferman Jr. and I cast the play from people we knew in our classes. We actually got a full roster of people who would join in such an anti-cow college activity. I had to have a stage manager, but it couldn't be Ferman Jr. He had to help me out with every detail of getting this play put on. Since the play had several pretty girls in it, and my brother thinking that I knew diddley about staging and he could do better, he signed on as stage manager.

We went to the Dean of Mississippi State and told him what we were up to. He agreed it would be a nice switch from all that mooing going on at cow college. So, we were set. We got to use Lee Hall Auditorium.

My brother took a shine to the young lady who was playing the sophisticated girl role in the play. Her name was Etta Mae and her father was an Education Professor at the college. They began dating and it got serious. Paul took her to Okolona to introduce her to our parents.

We had rehearsals and believe it or not I could tell that the play was going to be better than the two I appeared in during high school. The play did come off and ran three nights and had a big crowd of people. We had nice publicity from *The Reflector* and a couple of fraternities and sororities got behind it. So, the play came off without a hitch and we all felt like Broadway was next. What was next though was an invitation from the superintendent James Carpenter of Okolona High School for us to bring our play to Okolona. That we did and it was even a larger hit there. I simply couldn't believe that things had progressed this far so fast. Looking back, I can say that *Good Grief* was about as deep as those two plays I was in under Miss Zaina. That is saying something, being that it was my first play and was a portend of what would happen in the future with my plays.

One other thing was that Paul and Etta Mae got very thick as they say and almost got up to the alter. But something happened, who knows what, and the marriage did not come off. Etta Mae ended up marrying a fraternity brother of Paul's in 1951. Skip forward 50 years later around the year 2000. Paul was now a big Amway convert and was attending an Amway meeting somewhere in Mississippi and who should he run into? None other than Etta Mae. She was now a widow with grown children and grandchildren. She and Paul hooked back up and to everyone's surprise they married. She was his fourth wife, and he was her second husband.

Nothing ever happened to make *Good Grief* any more successful than it had been in Starkville and Okolona. It did, however, push me forward toward my writing career.

My parents died in the mid 1970's. We were the only Fitzgeralds who lived in Okolona. So, after Ruth and Everette passed on, I came back to arrange their funeral and sell the family home and definitively give up on Okolona. The next time I was in Okolona was about six or seven years later to attend your wedding. The event was on your father's farm and it was outdoors, if I remember correctly.

Ferman Jr. had left Mississippi State after our first year and transferred to a bible college near Atlanta Georgia. By this time, he had become a minister and officiated at your wedding. We were all grown by then. After Ferman Jr. left Mississippi State, I went to Mexico of all places. But that is another story which I will save till later.

Your wedding was the first time I was back in Okolona after the death of my parents. The next time I was there was in the early 90's when I was working on a film project in the Dothan, Alabama area. The producer's wife was from Ponotoc, Mississippi, which is 17 miles, more or less, from Okolona. When they heard that bit of information, they asked me to go with them as they were intending that weekend to visit her parents in Ponotoc. They said they would gladly take me back through Okolona. I took them up on their offer and away we went. I hadn't been in Okolona at that time for 30 or so years.

Okolona did not look well. It was sick and was fighting for its life. Most stores had been closed downtown and things looked more dead than alive. I ran into several people I knew. One of them told me Miss Zaina was in the local nursing home with Alzheimer and didn't recognize anyone. I asked my Ponotoc friends if they would take me to go see her. Even though she had terrified me when I was her student, I still thought I should at least go by and see her. We drove to the home and went inside. The first thing I saw was Miss Zaina sitting in a wheelchair. She had a smile on her face that would not go away. She did not recognize me. She just had that frozen smile on her face. It broke my heart to see such a powerful woman reduced to a vegetable. I took a photo of her and soon left. I was quite disturbed by this for quite some time. I was, never-the-less, glad that I had gotten to see her for one final time.

Then the last time I was in Okolona was about five years ago when you had arranged your family reunion. Unlike the Fitzgeralds, you had tons of local family. You invited me to be a part of it and I was extremely happy. I couldn't believe it, but you had five grown sons, and I got to see Ferman Jr. after years and years. Funny, we picked up as tough we had not seen one another for a weekend. He was the minister of a church in Amory which is a hop and skip from Okolona. Of course, that Sunday I had to go to his church and watch him preach. It was like being in a time machine to take all of this in. From the pulpit Ferman Jr. introduced me to the congregation. He told them that we had been inseparable friends all of our lives and that Jack went to Hollywood and he went to Jesus.

I certainly enjoyed meeting all of your sons and was amazed that each was so different from the other. They had families and I really enjoyed meeting them. Also, it was great to see others that I had known years and years ago.

I think I have rambled on far too long here. I just wanted to tell you how much I have appreciated knowing all of your family for all these years.

Take care and I look forward to your next Christmas card/newsletter. Be sure to tell everyone I send my best. Oh, by the way, I just turned 89. So that means Ferman Jr. is 88 too and you are 86. Can you believe that we are this old?

Cheers and very best to you.
Love, Jack

LETTER 3

SYLVIA

Dear Sylvia,

Thanks so much for showing me around your theatre. I spent a very pleasant hour viewing your facility. Not only is it a still functioning theatre, but one with a very interesting history. When you told me that it was a Vaudeville theatre in the 1920s, I could just imagine the stories it could tell. You say nowadays it is hard to keep the theatre going but it is worth the effort. I certainly second that.

I wish our get together could have been longer, but I was under a time constraint. I did however order a copy of my book *Paris Plays* to be sent to you. It contains eight of my plays which were originally produced by The Paris English Theatre in Paris, France.

I know when I told you about the book, you had numerous questions concerning how on earth did I start an English theatre in Paris and how did I manage to keep it going. I didn't have time to go into all of this with you in person, but I thought a copy of my book and this email to you might clear up a bit of your curiosity.

My educational background includes two years as an undergraduate at The University of Mexico in Mexico City, Mexico. I then finished my Bachelor of Art in English at Mississippi State College in Starkville. Next,

I received my master's degree in Spanish from Middlebury College in Vermont, which included a year of studies at The University of Madrid in Spain. This is a brief synopsis my educational endeavors and international studies.

My learning experiences prepared me well for my various teaching opportunities and later on the founding of the Paris English Theatre.

Upon my return from Madrid, I secured a teaching position at New York State University, in Plattsburg. During my second year, I was appointed faculty advisor for the Junior Year Abroad program to study at The University of Guadalajara in Mexico, for one semester. When the term was over, I did not want to return from sunny Guadalajara to the frozen tundra of Plattsburg. I applied for a semester's sabbatical to go to Paris and learn French in preparation for my PhD in Languages.

So, Sylvia, the truth of the matter is that I did not return to Plattsburg even after my sabbatical. Nor did I work on my PhD. Instead, I found a job teaching English as a foreign language and stayed in Paris to test my luck as a writer.

It had always been a dream of mine to become a writer since the age of 18, when I wrote my first play, *Good Grief.*

Being that I was in the capital of writers, I figured I would try to throw my hat into the ring. Paris had been the home of such great writers as Ernest Hemingway, Gertrude Stein, F. Scott Fitzgerald and many, many others. I was hoping I would find my muse in the city of lights.

As a means for supporting myself, I gave private English classes and they could be at rather irregular hours. One day while I was between classes, I walked through the area where the school was located. I noticed a group of people standing around outside of a café-theatre. I, being naturally curious, went over to see what was going on. A pleasant young British lady with a clipboard told me that a Canadian lady was producing a play and they were holding auditions. The production was N. F. Simpson's play, *The Resounding Tinkle.* She asked me if I wanted to try out for one of the roles. On a whim I agreed. I was told to wait until my name was called and then read for them. They asked me to hang around a bit. I said I couldn't because I had a class to teach but would be finished at 5:00 pm. They said that it was perfectly fine for me to return at that time.

After my class finished, I returned to the cafe-theatre. They wanted me to play the role for which I had read. This was an avant-garde play and it did not make much sense. The play had only three characters and they wanted me to play the solo male character. I talked with the producer and found her to be very pleasant. She was in Paris to establish an English-speaking theatre, hoping that there was money to be made from the endeavor.

So, we rehearsed and did our very best. The location where we presented the play was a café-theatre, which is a mixture of a bar and a theatre. We did ok but the lady lost her shirt and fled back to Canada. The people who ran the café-theatre asked me if we wanted to produce another play there. Impulsively I said yes. I had a one-act play I had written called *Killing Time*. The manager of the café-theatre didn't care as long as we brought in some customers for drinks.

So, we began rehearsals for *Killing Time*. It was a two-character play about an elderly lady and a young girl both are at the end of their ropes as far as life goes. They end up saving one another. I must say, even though it sounds interesting, it was rather turgid.

I found actors by putting an ad in the *International Herald Tribune*, the leading daily, English-language newspaper published in Paris. I found a young lady, who, with her husband and two-year-old, had come to Paris so her husband could work on his PhD in French Literature. The old lady was played by a one-woman show person who did Gertrude Stein shows. In it she portrayed life during the control of France by the Germans in World War II.

Finally, it was the night of dress rehearsal. Everyone was ready to go. However, a major problem developed. The actress playing the old lady did not show up. We called her landlady. She told us that Nancy had accepted an offer that morning to go to Brussels to do her one-woman show. That left us high and dry. So, what to do? I told everyone I would cry if I thought it would help. Since it wouldn't help, I had to do something. Mark, the PhD student whose wife was playing the young girl, said he would volunteer to put on the wig and play the part in drag. He said he knew the blocking and could read from a script.

I told him that I would certainly think it over. I then suggested that they go home and come back within an hour or so.

I went home and threw out much of my turgid play. I thought that everyone would laugh at us if we tried to have a serious play, especially with Mark, a very masculine man, who would not be accepted at face value as an old lady. I redid most of the old lady part to make it farcical rather than overly serious as it was at the present.

I went back to the theatre, and we rehearsed the new version. The next night we opened to a full crowd, mainly some of my English students. They loved Mark's rendition of the old lady.

Anyway, that is what we did. We turned the play into a farce. Where we had originally been booked to run two weeks, we went twelve weeks with big audiences at each performance.

Talk about making lemonade out of lemons, this was show business at its most powerful.

So, Sylvia, this is how The Paris English Theatre came about. After our second performance we went to a nearby restaurant to celebrate our having survived. We called ourselves the Paris English Theatre, a name that was active in the Paris theatre scene for over twenty years.

I hope this explains how I came to live in Paris and ended up running an English language theatre in Paris. When you get your copy of my book *Paris Plays*, be sure to read the opening introduction as it tells more about this dynamic group.

Cheers,

Jack

My first stage play.

LETTER 4

MOLLY

Dear Molly,

Recently your mom told me about you and Aaron getting engaged. I am so happy for the two of you and cannot wait to be a great, great uncle.

I don't know how much you know about our family. When I was your age, I had a lot of relatives alive and very active with one another. My grandmother lived with us in our home in Okolona. I don't know how much you know about her. My mother was her eldest daughter. In those times old people generally finished out their years living with their children. Nowadays, like for me, we live in an assisted living facility.

My grandmother Lilly was really something else. She was tough. She was French and was a very pretty woman up until her death. She had beautiful teeth, never having gone to the dentist a day in her life.

Her husband, my grandfather, Sargent Prentiss Howard, in his youth was an adventurous young man. He and some friends of his went into the mountains around Monterrey, Mexico in the 1880's. They were prospecting for gold and silver. They were doing okay but were attacked by Mexican bandits. Only my grandfather and a friend of his escaped the attack. The others were killed.

My grandfather and his friend quickly got out of Mexico and into Texas. They established a hardware store in San Antonio specializing in prospecting equipment.

My grandfather's friend had a sister by the name of Lucy. Over time Lucy and SP, as he was called, began courting and after a while were engaged. The people who knew my grandfather used SP. If they had called him Sargent people might think he was in the army. Even so, he was named after a very well-known Southern politician.

Marriage time was approaching for Lucy and SP. Lucy's brother arranged a bachelor's party trip for SP and his friends to St. Louis before he got married and settled down. Lucy told him to buy her a French hat to get married in.

SP and his buddies went to St. Louis and had a blowout of a time. On the last day my grandfather quickly tried to find a hat shop that sold French hats. He did find one to his relief. He went into the store and saw the most beautiful hat he had ever seen. Her name was Lilly and she was French. It was instant love on his part.

Three days later SP and Lilly got married. This of course busted up his friendship with his business partner. Lucy was terribly distraught. My grandfather and Lilly took off for the state of Washington where he got into the lumber business. Before that though, they went to Fulton, Mississippi, to live with his father who was a doctor. There my mother was born. After that they took off for the state of Washington. While living in the wilds of that state near a place called Wallaby's Wall, Lilly had a second girl which she named Ripple. Terrible luck intervened and Lilly came down with uremic poisoning. She was totally paralyzed on her right side.

Help was scarce in Walla Walla. Just a few Indian women were available to help. So, my grandfather decided to return to Mississippi and once again live with his father. SP became a banker, opening two banks in the area. Lilly through grit and determination managed to walk again even though her right side was paralyzed. That is why I say she was a tough lady. She even had three more children and lived to her late eighties.

So, Molly, I just thought a marriage story might be appropriate at this point in time with a marriage in your immediate future. My very best to you and Aaron.

Much love,
Uncle Jack

Maternal grandmother Lilly.

Maternal grandfather Sargent Prentiss Howard.

Mother and grandmother.

LETTER 5

BECKY

Dear Becky,

It's time for my monthly letter to you. Thank you for your email wishing me a happy 89th birthday. All in all, the day was quiet and simple. I received cards from family and friends, had a few phone calls and a few gifts. I know when I was a kid my birthday was a big event. However, once you pack on as many years as I have, birthdays seem to be all too frequent and are for the most part totally unbelievable.

One of the most unusual emails I got for my birthday was from the other Becky in the family who just also happens to be a doctor and whose mother also happened to be name Jenny. Unfortunately, the news my cousin Becky wrote was that her mother Jenny had passed away recently at the age of 103. It is strange that we have two Becky Fitzgeralds in the family, one on my mother's side and the other on my father's side. I don't think the two of you have ever met.

You are my brother Paul's daughter, Becky, and the other Becky is my Uncle Bob's daughter. Uncle Bob was my father Everette's brother. My father was the youngest of 11 children. Our family on my father's side was like a southern Gothic novel with tons of different intrigues and mysteries.

My father had ten brothers and sisters. All of them were southerners. Unfortunately, my father's father and mother died by the time he was two years old. Van, the oldest sibling, tried to raise some of the kids on his own but had to spread the rest out into the homes of family members who would take them.

My father at age two and his sister, Nanny Lou, age five, were given over to an aunt of theirs to raise, Aunt Mattie. Mattie had been married for only a short time, like a month or so, when her husband was struck by lightning and was killed. She lived on a farm on the outskirts of Egypt, Mississippi. She never remarried but devoted herself to raising Everette and Nanny Lou. Her source of income from her farm was raising and selling chickens, selling milk and butter and some baked goods. As you can imagine, times were hard for her and the kids.

Mattie sold the farm and moved to Okolona, a larger city seven miles away. She had thought there would be more opportunity for them in a town of 2,000 as opposed to Egypt's 350. The real reason she sold the farm was because an aunt of hers had died and left her the family home in Okolona.

So, this saga just goes on and on. Everette, around age six, was put to work to bring in some money. Aunt Mattie imported her chicken, butter, and baked goods business to Okolona. That was a bit more lucrative.

Everette was a scrappy child and due to his trying to excel at most things he attempted, he was called Grits, for his grit and determination.

Anyway, Grits went to school for two years and at the age of eight was hired as a call boy at the local railroad station. His job was to go to the two rooming houses and wake up the engineers so they could get ready to work on their trains. Grits, who never had any other job, worked for the railroad his entire life. He went from call boy up to ticket selling and Railway Express, the shipping arm of the Railroad business. He tried to go to school and work when he could. He got as far as the eighth grade but had to abandon school and dedicate himself to putting food on the table for his aunt and Nanny Lou.

Their house in Okolona was not in great shape. It wasn't until Grits, later known as Pete, began working full time at the railroad in his early 20s, that he could afford to fix the place up a bit. The house was built before the Civil War in the 1850's. During that war it served as a hospital, then later for Yankee soldiers during the occupation. After the civil war, the house was turned into a girls' finishing school, which was run by Mattie's two spinster aunts, Miss Kitty and Miss Laura. The women ran the school until old age forced them to retire. The place was desperately in need of repairs and its fashionable decor totally went downhill. The two sisters had rocking chairs on the front porch and rocked themselves into oblivion. Aunt Laura outlasted Kitty and it was she who gave the house to Mattie.

Meanwhile those ten siblings of my father were, for the most part, married. They begat children and had their own sagas apart from Everette and Nanny Lou. One of them was my Uncle Bob's very sweet daughter Rebecca or Becky Fitzgerald or Dr. Fitzgerald to be exact. I was really glad to get her card but sad to hear that her mother had passed away.

Anyway, I'll end this letter here and will write you another one next month. I'll try to include some interesting family tidbits.

Take care and know how proud of you I am.

Love,
Uncle Jack

LETTER 6

LEROY

Dear Leroy,

What a fun experience talking with you on the phone the other day. I really couldn't believe that we were talking. It sounded so much like we just took up from where we left off over 50 years ago when we were Army buddies stationed on Okinawa.

I guess we have to score another hit for Facebook. I rarely am on there but use it from time to time to promote my books. During one of those times I saw a musician with your name but he was young and even looked like you. I investigated and found out that it was your son. I got into contact with him and before I knew it, he had provided me with your telephone number. He said that over the years you had mentioned my name to him many times, so he felt like he knew who I was.

I called you and honestly, it was like being in a time machine. Your voice sounded exactly the way I remembered it all those years ago. I believe both of us left Okinawa in 1955. You and I really were what you would call Army buddies. I guess when you are thousands of miles away from home, and like us, on a small island in the middle of nowhere, you have to have a best friend to talk over life with. You count the days until you can leave.

We certainly did that. You told me about your background in the New England area and I told you about my hometown of Okolona, Mississippi.

One thing though, and I guess it is normal, we didn't keep up a correspondence once we got out of the Army and went our separate ways. We might have swapped a letter or two, but life overcomes us and we began new lives and interests. You got married and had children. I never married.

The thing that knocked my socks off in our conversation the other day was that you told me you actually had been to Okolona, Mississippi. You told me how you and your wife made a trip to Okolona just to check to see if I still lived there. You asked around and was told that I didn't live there anymore and also that my parents had died, and I had no local connections. You then went to Okolona's small public library and found that I had written several books, which they had on display, something like small town boy makes good. You said you were disappointed you did not find me or any person who could furnish you with any information concerning me. You said that you read the back cover of the book where they always give information about the author and found out that I was an author that had lived in Paris, France, and established The Paris English Theatre there.

It was great that we did get back together after all those years. As I said on the telephone the other day, it was like old times, except for over 50 years later.

Leroy, one thing for sure, we now know where to find one another. Those wonderful memories we shared on that little island got explored once again and it was truly just wonderful.

Take care and the best to your family.
Your Army buddy, Jack of Okolona

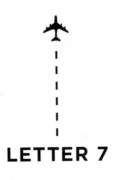

LETTER 7

BOB

Dear Bob,

Thanks so much for your letter. I am glad you got a copy of my book *Contessa* and now have finished reading it. I really do appreciate all the compliments you threw my way about the book. You stated that you especially enjoyed the last third of the book which takes place in Cuba during the Fidel Castro revolution in 1958. You said you were intrigued by all the adventures the main character had during such a tumultuous time. You then asked me how I ended up in Cuba and in such a set of circumstances. So, I will try to explain it to you.

Like most things, life is not simple, but a string of incidents fueled by fate. In my case it all started with my getting an undergraduate degree. The first year I went to Mississippi State University with my lifelong friend Ferman Jr. After that first year, Ferman Jr. went to Atlanta to attend a religious school to become a minister. I went to Mexico City and attended the University of Mexico. Then I went into the Army for three years. After getting out of the Army, I attended Mexico City College in Mexico City for a year. Then for my fourth year I went back to Mississippi State for a year and graduated with a major in English and a minor in Spanish. I hope you're still with me. I have lived a rather convoluted life and this part of my education proves it.

While getting ready to graduate from Mississippi State I had to start thinking about what to do with my life. I was an English major and so what did that qualify me for? As best I could figure it meant that I would teach school. Through the placement office at Mississippi State, I applied for several jobs as a high school English teacher. The best offer I could come up with was twenty-seven hundred dollars a year at the high school in Clarksdale, Mississippi. The salary was adequate at the time because the year was 1957. My mother had always wanted me to get a good government job at the post office. That did not appeal to me in any sense of the word. I was seriously considering the position in Clarksdale until I had a talk with a Cuban student attending Mississippi State who lived next door to me in the dormitory. I explained the situation to him, and he said I ought to go to Havana, Cuba, where I could teach school at a private English language school and for sure make more money than at Clarksdale High. Besides, Havana had to be more exciting than Clarksdale.

I graduated from Mississippi State, turned down the Clarksdale job and was on my way to Havana, Cuba. My mother was very disappointed. My father was elated as he had self-taught himself Spanish and thought that my going to the lovely island of Cuba would be a top rank adventure.

I took a bus from Okolona and after a couple of changes ended up in Miami, Florida. From there I went to Key West and from Key West, I could take Cubana Airlines to Havana for ten dollars. So, one ticket please and away I went.

Havana was like no place else. It was all party, party, party all the time. Tourists came here by the droves to sin and drink rum and be like they couldn't at home.

Prostitution was a big business in Havana. My first week I met a prostitute named Yolanda who tried to offer her services to me at one of the ocean side cafes but soon found that I was gay and not good client material. Instead, she bought me a beer and we became fast friends. She found me a decent place to live and before I knew it, I was indeed teaching English at the Oxford School of English.

At the school I was assigned some classes and my name was to be Mr. Lamb. I was assigned this name because of Charles Lamb, the writer. Everyone teaching there had a fictitious name of classical origin. Debbie Schwartz, a friend of mine, converted this to Miss Shakespeare. She explained to me the reason was because the turnover of teachers was so frequent in their faculty. Besides the students couldn't pronounce their teachers' real names. Hence, I taught with Charles Dickens, Gertrude Stein, Ernest Hemingway, etc.

Before long, there was the rumblings of a revolution led by Fidel Castro. It was terrible and a lot of people lost their lives. Foreign teachers after the revolution were accused of spreading anti-revolutionary propaganda. They were actually shooting teachers as well as Batista soldiers to the tune of over 500 a day. People attended these executions as though they were entertainment.

I was very scared. One day a Jeep pulled up in front of where I was staying. Some rebel soldiers got out, told me to leave and not take anything with me. I was sure they were taking me to the stadium. They didn't. They took me to the airport and put me on a plane for Key West. I made it back to the USA alive.

All of these experiences I used in the last third of my book *Contessa*. The main character in the book is a far cry from me and my life, being that the plot concerns a young man going to Havana for a sex change and who gets caught up in the revolution. I used all my experiences there in the book.

So, Bob, there you have it. I did manage to get out of this experience alive and to tell about it in a book and this letter to you. Again, I am so glad that you like the book.

Very best to you, your friend,
Jack

Jack with Cuban Rebels in 1958.

LETTER 8

SCOTT

Dear Scott,

Thanks for the interview. I am pleased with how well we got along. I do think that your interview will stoke interest in the production of my play locally. In our interview, I told you all about my background as a writer in Paris, Los Angeles, and in the most recent years, here in Palm Springs.

Just as we were finishing the interview for your magazine *Bottom Line*, I mentioned that I also was one of the founders of the LGBTQ Center here in Palm Springs. You said that you would like to hear more but unfortunately you had to leave due to a prior commitment. I told you that I would write a brief overview of this particular avenue of my life. I am glad you will be doing a follow up article on our Center. From what I write you here, I think you will be able to prepare for another interview based solely on the Desert Pride Center. When I moved from Los Angeles to Palm Springs in the late seventies with the intention of retiring from writing, I unfortunately did not know any people locally. I had a couple of friends who lived here but everyone else were strangers. I soon found out that most people retired to the Palm Springs area to eat, drink, and hit the bars and restaurants. That was okay for them but not for me. I had lived a very active life as a writer and did not subscribe to the eat drink and be merry regimen.

In West Hollywood, where I lived before moving to Palm Springs, there was a very large gay center. They had classes as well as a full-sized theater where they presented very good productions and stage events. I was not an active participant. I think I probably went there four times during my fifteen years in West Hollywood. Two of my visits there were as a guest speaker concerning two books of mine. The first was *Contessa*, which was about a transsexual and the second *Viva La Evolución*, a satirical novel with a Spanish title but written in English.

When I moved to Palm Springs from Los Angeles, I just took it for granted that a LGBTQ center already existed. To my big surprise, no such place existed. Instead, there were about a dozen clubs that catered to different aspects of LGBTQ lifestyles. There was a Lesbian dining club group, a group for elderly gay men, a suicide prevention group, and several other social groups such as AARP and AA fellowships. This was all well enough but there was no central location in which these different communities could participate such as the center in Los Angeles.

Life went on with my limited social outlet for a while. One day the magazine *Bottom Line,* a gay publication, carried an article about a couple of people who were studying the possibility of establishing a LGBTQ center. They were having a public meeting at the Mizelle Senior Center to discuss the matter. I attended along with about 30 others. A man and a woman with social organizational experience were very good at stoking interest in such a project. They divided the attendees into committees to get together and talk over different aspects of such a project. I was on the social committee, which was to come up with ideas for possible activities at such a center. I volunteered to teach Spanish, French, screenplay writing, and writing the story of one's life. Others volunteered to teach sign language, create discussion groups and various other social activities.

The meeting ended with the woman and man telling us that they would get back to us shortly about putting our plans into action.

Months went by and I heard nothing and so I called the lady who organized the event to see what was going on. She said that they were working on things and that it was all very slow. All of a sudden, I felt like the project was going down the tubes and that more than likely others got to this point but never beyond it. Hence, there was still no LGBTQ Center in Palm Springs.

In my writing career I had written several plays which actually were produced. Most people would talk about producing a play, but it never saw opening night. When I started the Paris English Theater, I realized that to actually make a play come off that you had to force it to happen. So, I told the lady I would host a meeting if she and the gentleman would come. The difference between my meeting and their meeting was that I set dates for things to happen. As it turned out we had a board of eight people, each in charge of a specific activity and with a specific date, which was two weeks away. I said at that meeting we would go forward as an established center. In two weeks we had installed a telephone as well as filed for nonprofit status.

The only thing lacking was a name for the center. We each gave our suggestions and ended up with our name being The Desert Pride Center. We all were in agreement on the name and I suggested that immediately we distribute it out as the center's main contact.

A board member asked me where I got all of my energy for doing this project. I told her that it was exactly like putting on a play. You could talk about it till the cows came home and it would never happen. Action not words was the way it happened. I had experience putting on plays in Paris at the Paris English Theatre. The next thing was to have a fund raiser so we could rent a place to call home. I suggested a local gay bar and I would get some of my actor friends, several from the popular film Sordid Lives, as well as Kaye Ballard to come and sell memberships at $25 to a $100. We raised nearly $1,500.

My cohorts, at least half of them, wanted to have a retreat and make up a boiler plate set of rules and regulations. I said that was the way to do the project in.

Mike, one of the board members, found us an ex-dentist's office. With lots of effort we managed to open it as our first LGBTQ center. I was in charge of programs. I taught Spanish, French, screenwriting and even instituted a course called Drag 101, a night course on how to be a drag queen. That was run by two guys, who showed up one day to help out before our grand opening. They said they dressed up for Halloween and were known as Bella da Ball and Honey Dew Melon. They did a wonderful job. We had a great opening day and the Center was finally officially opened. The event was covered by the local TV media and so, at long last, Palm Springs did have a LGBTQ center. I organized potluck dinners and other events for people to come to the center and find friends in classes and events.

I remained on the board for three years but finally had to resign to get back to having a life of my own and writing more books. In the intervening years this center was takeover by another group and is now a well-established part of the Palm Springs community.

So, Scott, perhaps you will do a story on the origins of our local community center for LGBTQ.

I look forward to seeing you again.

Cheers,

Jack

LETTER 9

BARRY

Dear Barry,

Thanks for your email. I was pleasantly surprised to hear that your grandmother has a grandson who is getting ready to go to college. She mentioned that you were interested in becoming a writer and you had some questions for me about the profession. Your grandmother was one of my closest friends when I was a youngster in Mississippi. In fact, her brother, Ferman, was my best friend. To think I am writing to a third-generation friend is interesting and exciting.

I will certainly be pleased to answer your questions and offer some advice on how to go about becoming a writer. I will be glad to pass along some important information as you enter this line of work.

First of all, there is no fixed way of joining the writing profession. It is necessary to get a good four-year education. You can major in creative writing but that is no guarantee that you will be able to jump into the writing profession. After you finish four years of Liberal Arts, you must take advantage of every opportunity to gain further education and experiences in life. I personally believe that in order to write you have to do two things: experience as many adventures in life as you can and read and do research to make sure your writing is authentic and factual.

As you must know, I went to Mississippi State for my freshman and senior years. Then between those two years, I went to the University of Mexico in Mexico City. I taught English as a second language to bring in some cash to support having a roof over my head. Later, I went to Middlebury College in Vermont where I completed a master's degree in Spanish. In addition to taking classes at Middlebury I completed a year of classes at the University of Madrid.

Upon completion of the master's program, I then taught at Wake Forrest College in Winston Salem, North Carolina. Then I taught Spanish at New York State University in Plattsburg, New York, where, for one year I was the head of their Junior Year Abroad Program in Guadalajara, Mexico. Soon after that I went to Paris to try to kickstart my career in writing.

In order to support myself in Paris, I taught at a private language school. After three years there, I was promoted to director. This was a wonderful opportunity as I was in charge of over 1,000 students. As you can see, I had a lot to write about.

One day the president of the school asked if I wanted to go to Cambridge University in England to learn all about a new method of teaching a foreign language especially geared to students of the English language. I jumped at the opportunity, and I spent a summer attending classes at this very famous university. I met people from all over the world. One of my most interesting experiences concerned a young lady from Albania. I know that sometimes in Paris I would listen to foreign radio stations just to see what was going on in the rest of the word. At that time the Soviet Union was the big scare and they had radio stations that had communist propaganda programs such as *Radio Moscow, Radio East Berlin,* and *Radio Tirana* from Albania. I was interested in listening to this station because my brother had married an Albanian lady. The announcers at these stations spewed nonstop propaganda. One of my favorite newscasters was from Albania. She had a syrupy voice and I wondered about what she would be like in person. Much to my surprise, this very lady attended the same courses I did for the summer. We got to be great friends, along with many other interesting people. We would get her to do an example of her propaganda broadcast to show us how she did it. We were all fascinated.

As you can see, just from what I have written to you in this email, the things one could write about. I have written my experiences into my eight published books, my stage plays, and my screenplays. So, what I am telling you, Barry, is that you have to have something interesting to write about first and foremost if you want to be a writer. So go out and have some adventures, meet interesting people, and then write about them. Your writing will just flow.

I hope this letter will be of help to you. Tell Becky that I send my best and I do wish you the very best, Barry. Let me know how things progress for you.

My very best to you,
Jack Fitzgerald

LETTER 10

LAURA

Dear Laura,

Thank you for the birthday card that was made in India. It was a painting of the Taj Mahal. I must say my mind went back over fifty years when I was in that area. An Indian Fakir told me I would return to India but I had no idea that it would be via you and a beautiful birthday card celebrating my eighty-ninth birthday.

I know what you are thinking right at this moment, "What in the world was he doing in India?" Knowing your curiosity, I will gladly tell you.

In the 1960s one of the most celebrated films was Mike Todd's *Around the World in Eighty Days*. I had read the book when I was young and when this movie reached the screen, I was nothing short of very excited to see it.

In the time that passed after my seeing the film, my brain started thinking about taking my own version of *Around the World in Eighty Days*. I discussed it with four friends of mine, all teachers. The more I talked about such an idea, the more I was convinced that we should do this. I went to see a lady named Carol at a local travel agency and she was super helpful from the start. Instead of laughing at me, she thought it was a wonderful idea. I asked her if it were possible for her to give me a ballpark cost of such a trip. She asked me to wait a few minutes while she calculated the price. I was sure the total would exceed my budget. After a few minutes, she looked up at me and smiled and told me the basic cost would be $2,200.00. I was delighted because with help from my parents, I could afford such a trip. Once I had an estimate for the trip, I approached my friends and got their okays to join in the adventure. So, for most of 1967 the dream was becoming more of a reality.

The five of us got together and worked out places that we wanted to visit. These were limited to Paris, London, Berlin, and about fifteen more 'gotta-see' places. We figured that other cities would provide interesting side adventures. The day finally came for our five intrepid world adventurers to set out on our around the world experience.

We did not have to wait very long for the first adventure to set upon us. We left Los Angeles dressed in sport coats, ties, and big smiles. We boarded Braniff Airlines for the flight from Los Angeles to Lima, Peru. We were to change planes in Lima immediately upon arrival to then board a small prop jet to take us to Iquitos, Peru. This town was at the headwaters of the Amazon and one thing I had always wanted to do was go down the Amazon. Hence, we were in this wide and powerful river that day. The thing that turned this into an adventure was the problem that our luggage was lost and had not made it to Lima and certainly not Iquitos. We were dressed like missionaries. We hooked up with our tour guide, a spry young Indian. The first thing I noticed about him was a big scar on his left leg. I asked him what that was. I know the others would not ask him, but I am rather nosy, so I posed the question. The answer was that he had been bitten by a big snake. He had just mentioned the word I hate: snakes. So, with our Indian guide we got into a home-made boat large enough for the six of us and away we went down the Amazon.

We were headed to some Indian village located on a tributary in the dense jungle. Mind you, we were still wearing our dress clothes that we wore when we left Los Angeles.

We got to this village where the people painted things on their faces and wore straw hula skirts, both men and women. This lasted longer than we thought because we could not leave this village due to heavy rain. So, we had to stay there with the straw skirted people and join them for dinner which consisted mostly of meat. They used blowguns to hit monkeys in the trees and they would fall to ground. Then a tribe member would go get it and throw it into a big pot with lots of water in it. They built a fire around the pot where the monkeys were boiled for about three or so hours. Once the monkey was done, they would all start reaching into the dark, murky water of the pot and tear off some flesh and eat it. They asked us to join them. Even though I was hungry, I would not eat the first bit of that monkey meat. Two of our group did but I was not one of them. The proverbial answer about how it tasted was, "It tastes like chicken."

Sometime later the rain stopped, and we were able to leave. On our way out of the dense foliage we indeed did see several snakes. I couldn't wait to get back to civilization.

We made it back to Lima, still wearing our going-away costumes from Los Angeles. We all had a rather ripe smell. The airline company provided some new clothing and finally located our bags. They had gone to Frankfurt, Germany by mistake. Once we got that straightened out, we continued on our world tour by going to Chile, Argentina, and Brazil. Most of those experiences were mild adventures. In other words, fun rather than stressful.

In my planning of this trip, one of the areas we wanted to visit was the Middle East by visiting Israel, Jordan, Egypt, and Iran. We had to get special visas to get through the Mandelbaum Gate in Israel and Jordan and a very special visa to get into Egypt. All was set except the Six Day war broke out. By the time we got to Israel, the war had finished. The Mandelbaum Gate had been blown to smithereens and one could just walk through as there was no passport control there. Egypt had partially been overrun by the Israelis and so we were not able to go there. We mainly saw the aftermath of the war and that was very interesting. We went from Israel to Turkey and continued on. I did not mention London, Paris, Berlin, etc. because our experiences there were normal.

We went to Turkey and Iran and flew from Iran to Kabul in Afghanistan. We quickly found out that this was a very poor country. We stayed at the finest hotel just across from the Royal Palace which was not even up to Motel 6 standards. We ate in their finest restaurants. Breakfast consisted of green scrambled eggs and some meat, which we had no idea what it was. Lunch was a chicken salad sandwich, which was barely edible. Diner was roasted chicken which had very little meat on its bones. Right down the middle of Kabul was an open stream where people bathed and gathered to talk. We went on a walking tour of downtown Kabul, the capital city, and in the best parts were fur shops. That seemed to be the big business. I was the only one who wanted to go into one of the small shops on the main street. The step into the place was a concrete block. I stepped on the block and the smell of the interior hit my nose and I went backward on that block and fell into the open sewer which ran through downtown. I had waste all over me. The employees of the fur shop noticed me and brought out jugs of water and tried to wash the filth off me in the hot Afghan sun. It didn't work and just dried too quickly. I was a mess. We returned to our hotel and I showered as best as I could to get back to decency.

We were not sorry to leave Kabul. I do hope it has changed for the better in all these years. From Kabul we flew to Lahore, Pakistan.

We found Lahore to be a pleasant British colonial city with lots of palm trees and nice avenues. We were told that for our own safety and to help us we needed to hire the service of a guide. I don't exactly know how we came up with this particular guide but in thinking back, I believe he had something to do with the family who ran the hotel where we were staying. We enjoyed his services in touring Lahore. One day the guide asked us if we wanted to go see the cave people. He said that they were a group of people who lived in huts and ran stores out of their caves. It sounded very adventurous to me. The next day we went with the guide. Two of our group did not want to go so that left four in his large car. Away we went and the first big surprise was that we arrived at a big gate that had a sign on it that read, "Past this point you no longer will be protected by the Pakistani Army or government. Enter at your own risk." Before we knew it, our guide had us past the gate.

In this new territory were people who dressed in a kind of long robe and turbans. Some people were stretched out on cots under shade trees. They were working on the manufacture of armaments, rifles, pistols, and you name it. They also sold cocaine and all sorts of rugs. One thing in common was that they looked dangerous. They offered us tea with the little cups on a swinging tray. The caves were where they stored their armaments. They would take us inside and try to sell rifles, or a pistol or some drugs. The women were cooking over an open fire and looked very servile. We had tea with them, and they seemed very friendly. They were not offended that we did not buy a gun or some drugs. I told our guide that maybe we should slowly make our way out of the place. He agreed even though he had a couple of people out there who were cousins of his. He didn't seem to be fearful of these people. We just did not feel safe at all. Our nerves were on edge from this until we were back on the other side of that warning fence. Today I believe that these people would be the Taliban.

To calm us down, our guide went back and got the two guys who didn't go to the tribal area. He took us to the American air base located in Peshawar where there was not very much to see. The one thing there was the American Strategic Air Command air base. The guide took us up to the gate and said we were American tourists on a round-the-world-trip. We were welcomed and taken to the non-commissioned officer's club where we had hamburgers and milk and were offered beer if we wanted it.

That was quite a change from our visit in the tribal zone near Peshawar.

The next day our guide told us was our Waterloo. This was the day that we were to go from Pakistan to India and pass through a war zone. We knew that we were going to face some problems because at that time Pakistan and India were in hostilities with one another. With our luggage, we were dropped off by our guide at the frontier. We were interrogated by the Pakistani Army officers. Mainly they wanted to know why we wanted to go to India. We had to tell them it was only so we could continue our trip. We pretended we were not much interested in India. After a while, something was decided, and we were told we could leave and walk through no-mans land to India. They told us not go get off the pathway because the area was mined. So, with our suitcases we waddled through the war zone on that path that led from Pakistan to India. We were told to wave a flag to the Indians. If they waved back to us, we could proceed to India. So, we got to the middle, waved the flag and got a flag wave back. We were quite relieved. We picked up our baggage and walked on that path into India. Once we got there, servants ran out and took our luggage and guided us to a waiting car. The driver was a woman who had been informed of our coming by the guide which she said was a cousin of hers.

Away we went.

The lady driver took us to the first Indian town nearest the border and we registered there. The next day we were on our way to continue with our trip. We had to make it to Calcutta to catch a plane to Thailand. Things did not happen as planned and so we stayed in Calcutta for two days extra because our plane did not arrive.

I had never seen so many people. We were supposed to just land there and continue on to places like Varanasi, where they burn the dearly departed on funeral pyres, and later on to the Taj Mahal. We also were to only stop over in Calcutta and then continue to Thailand. We were told by the airline that our connection was not available, and we had to stay in Calcutta. We later learned that the plane we were to fly on had crashed and we were to wait for a replacement. We did find Calcutta interesting from the standpoint of cows walking everywhere. Truly they had the run of the mill. I was walking in a building up to the second floor and ran into a cow coming down from the second floor. The cow looked at me and I had to back into the wall and wait for her to pass me by. Things are not sanitary because all these loose cows do not have any potty control. So, watch your step.

One of the things I had wanted to see in Malaysia was the snake temple. Even though I loathe snakes, I couldn't believe that the place was covered with snakes. Yes, indeed, I saw many, many snakes there. They all seemed to be sleeping. We were told that they came there and slept and rested for a season and then all two thousand snakes would return from whence they had come. We did not stay long in the snake temple.

The trip around the world was a great experience or I should say a wonderful collection of adventures. It ended up taking eighty-four days rather than the planned eighty. Also, one member of our troop left early. He said he was over-traveled and left us in Osaka, Japan to fly directly back to the United States.

The world has changed a lot since those days but think I was lucky to have a sense of the world at the time.

I assure you that when you bought that card printed in India you would not get such a long-winded reply. Thanks again for the card and for awakening my memories.

Love,
Jack

LETTER 11

LINDA

Dear Linda,

Thanks for the beautiful birthday card. You are one of the few people who actually will go through the ritual of buying a stamp, going to a postal pick-up site, and send your card on the way to its recipient. I know my mother always thought of you as her favorite niece and I can second that by claiming you to be my favorite cousin.

Your card got me to thinking about my mother a lot, your Aunt Ruth. In the 1970s I lived in Paris with my roommate Ken. My mother at that time had gone blind and she was a diabetic, having to take a shot of insulin every morning. At that time my mother lived with her sister Ripple in Houston. My brother Paul, his wife and four children would visit her every so often, but I was five thousand miles away in Paris, France chasing a writing muse.

The last time I was home I stayed for a month. My mother, being recently widowed, had no way to communicate with her family and friends. She had beautiful handwriting (mine is terrible) but being blind she no longer could write letters to people. She told me soon after I arrived that she had certain friends and family to whom she owed letters to and wanted me to write to them. I got the idea of teaching her to type. I had to learn how to type with a blind keyboard when I was in high school so not seeing the keyboard should not be a problem. I sat her down at my father's Underwood typewriter and away we went

I followed the system shown in a typing book I bought. The first few days we did exercises with various letter groups. My aunt said I was pushing her much too hard. I told her that was the only way she would ever learn.

During most of my time there with my mother we did those drills until she knew the keyboard. One day I told her to put a sheet of paper into the typewriter. Once it was ready to go, I had her type the words "Dear Elsie" (her sister-in-law). I told her then to type a sentence. That she did. I told her to write another one. Then I told her to say goodbye as she usually did in her letters. I told her to take the sheet of paper out of the typewriter and informed her that she had written her first letter. I had only one week to go in my visit and I wanted her to be able to enter the world of letter writing before I left.

So during that last week, she got braver and wrote letters to just about everybody. By the time I left, she was typing like a secretary. My family was absolutely amazed that at her age and condition that she did so well. Before I left Houston, I bought her a portable typewriter so she had a machine of her own to get used to. I returned to Paris and soon began receiving letters from her. Not short ones but long ones.

Ken was so impressed that he said we should invite her to come and visit us for a while. My going to see her was pretty much not easily done due to distance and my financial situation. We are talking about the days before email and the handwritten letter was king.

Her sister thought such an idea was impossible due to her being blind and flying all the way on Air France from Houston to Paris. My mother had enough of her French mother in her to take us up on our invitation. So, believe it or not in April of that year she boarded Air France and with the help of a sympathetic crew made it to Charles de Gaulle airport in Paris. A student of mine had volunteered to take Ken and me to the airport to receive her. It was one wonderful meeting the four of us had. My student had a beard and she wondered who he was. We told her it was Jean Pierre, a student of mine. She gave him a big hug and he said in mangled English, "Welcome Madam Ruth to Paris". We made our way to his car and off we went to our apartment. Mamma was at home immediately. As I mentioned before, Mamma was a diabetic, type one. She had mastered how to measure her insulin blind and then give herself the shot. Ken volunteered to give her the shot but, in her arm. She generally gave the shot in her leg but it truly needed a rest Ken said. Ken would faint if anyone with a needle approached him but somehow he was great at giving Mamma her insulin. So that became one less problem to deal with.

We took Mamma to a nearby hair salon so she could have a French look. We bought her some dresses and some perfume.

Ken and I soon were on vacation from teaching and we decided for the three of us to take a trip in his Volkswagen. So off we went for two weeks of fun and frolicking.

We ate at many different restaurants in France, Switzerland, Italy, Spain and Portugal. One time in a French restaurant Ken was eating raw oysters with gusto. I wouldn't touch them. Mamma had never eaten one but she dared to eat one of Ken's. One time in southern France we ate at an outdoor restaurant. Ken and I were having an aperitif. Mamma had never touched alcohol as far as I knew. All of a sudden, she asked me for a puff of my cigarette. I was obliged to let her try. I thought she would not like the cigarette. She not only had it but had a drink of my wine. In Switzerland we were in the Alps region and were staying an Alpine-type lodge. Mamma got up one morning and opened up the shuttered window and even though she could not see all of nature's beauty she was aware of it. She let out a big lung of fresh air and asked if this is what paradise felt like.

We were in Chamonix, a big ski resort town in France near the Swiss border. The air was crisp and very refreshing. Mamma stretched out her arms and said that she felt like a young girl. I can safely say she looked like a young girl.

We continued toward Spain and we stopped overnight in Marseilles, France. The town was overloaded with tourists. We looked for a place stay. Several places were too expensive for us. Mamma was sitting in the car waiting for us to return from our search for a room. She informed me that she had to pee something awful. We didn't know what to do.

We saw down the block a hotel with a big garish sign. It didn't matter. We headed towards it with Mamma. We went inside and asked the rather overly dressed and perfumed lady who seem to run the place if my mother could use the restroom. I told her that my mother was blind and it was an emergency. The lady said we could use the facility. She said she would take mamma and we could stay in the reception area. The lady then took Mamma off to the restroom while we cased the place. We noticed that men came in and out of the place and that women would greet men downstairs and then take them upstairs. Before long, we looked at one another and said under our breath that this was a whorehouse, a kind of nice one though. The lady appeared with Mamma, who looked all rested and satisfied. She was hanging on to the woman when we came back. The lady said that Mamma had told her that we were looking for a room but that we were having no luck as the town was packed due to some event. She then said that she had one big room for the three of us and as far as restaurants go, she added, that their restaurant was adequate and that we would not go hungry. Ken and I saw a good deal. But we worried about Mamma finding out that she was about to spend the night in a French whorehouse. We decided we would not tell her. Anyway, we had a great time that evening at that place.

The women of the night treated Mamma as though she were a queen. She ate up every minute of it. We said not a word nor did anyone else about where she was. When dinner came it was okay and nothing fancy. We ordered some wine. The Madam who had helped Mamma told us that she would have to charge us for the wine. She brought a bottle of wine. We hadn't thought of a whole bottle rather than just a glass. The Madam told us to drink what we wanted and she would pro rate the price. Anyway, Ken and I were having such a good time we just finished the bottle, with Mamma having a small glass. The girls sang some songs and Mamma really enjoyed herself.

The next morning when we came down for breakfast, the Madam presented us with the bill. We were charged for an entire bottle of wine, which we had consumed. Anyway, she did not try to overcharge us. And we did get a bargain there. Mamma hugged all of them before we left, and we got a wonderful send off. Mamma never knew that she spent the night in a whorehouse.

We stayed in a castle in Spain, a chateau in a French wine vineyard in France and did all sorts of things in our two weeks. When we got back to Paris, Mamma got out her portable typewriter and wrote up a one-page review of her trip. Once finished she named her article *Seeing Paris Blind*. She made copies and sent them to family and friends. She also sent a copy to the Okolona Messenger, the local newspaper in the town where she lived all of her married life. The paper published it and Mamma felt like a celebrity with all her friends and relatives talking about her having the experience of a lifetime. She said that she had to wait until she was 74 years old to really live. I was glad she had this experience and really tasted life at its best for she died about six months after returning to Houston.

So, you will know a bit more about my mother Ruth. I will attach her review called *Seeing Paris Blind*.

Cheers, and my very best to you,
Jack

A BRIEF REVIEW
OF OUR TRIP

BY RUTH FITZGERALD

Summer, 1973

We left Paris on Thursday morning July 12, 1973, and returned Sunday afternoon, August 13, 1973. The trip included France, Switzerland, Italy, Monaco and Spain. Highlights of the trip included: visits to Chateaux and the wine producing area of Burgandy in France. Then on to Switzerland and Geneva, a city of fountains and flowers. From Geneva to Italy via the Alps and a tunnel connecting the two countries. A two week stay on the Riviera, principally in Nice but including the Principality of Monaco and the fashionable Riviera cities of Cannes, St. Raphaël and St. Tropez. Visits were made to the world-famous casinos in Monte Carlo, Nice and Cannes. A side visit was made to a perfume factory in Grasse which is near Nice. The factory, Fragonard, produces from tons of flowers grown in the area the oils used to make the better-known French perfumes. One can buy the perfumes (but not under their trade names) for a fraction of their regular price. While in Nice, the annual flower carnival took place and there were floats decorated entirely in flowers. From Nice we went South to Marseilles and from there to the Pyrenees and into Spain where we spent five days in Barcelona. Barcelona is a shopper's paradise as well as a beautiful city and seaport. From Barcelona we went to the province of Aragon in Northern Spain of which Zaragoza is the capital. From there we went to Olite, Spain and spent a night in a 12th century castle. The Spanish government has made it possible on a limited basis for tourists to live the life of a feudal king in some of its ancient castles and we were fortunate enough to get in on this. There were only ten rooms for tourists and it was like living in a museum. The beds and great canapies over them and the furniture was all antique. From this experience we proceeded on to the beautiful Basque Country and the city of San Sebastian, Spain. The scenery is reminiscent of the Swiss Alps and the area is perhaps one of the quaintest in Europe. From there we continued to Pau, France, which is at the foot of the Pyrenees. It is an ancient city with a castle and a main street which is actually a balcony on which one promenades and views the tall Pyrenees in the distance. From Pau we went to Lourdes where Sainte Bernadette lived and the water brought forth through a vision she encountered with the Virgin Mary is supposed to have curative powers. All of us drank and bathed in the water. From there we proceeded to Auch in Southern France where one of the best restaurants in the country is located. We ate there and had a memorable night. From Auch we headed north to the town of Cahors, France which is a wine growing area of which the wine is so highly regarded that very little of it is even exported from the region. The city itself has many interesting bridges and castles dating from the Middle Ages. From Cahorskwe continued north to the valley of the Loire which is famous for the most beautiful castles and Chateaux in France. On the way we made a brief stopover in Limoges, a city which famous for its fine bone china. In Blois, we spent the night in a hotel on the edge of the river Loire. The city is very quaint and looks architecturally as it did two hundred years ago. From Blois we returned to Paris and as we saw the Eiffel Tower in the distance, we knew that as all things must eventually come to a close, we were lucky that Paris with all its history, charm and beauty was our final destination.

Ken in the kitchen.

LETTER 12

DAVID

Dear David,

Thanks for your email and letting me know that you had bought a copy of my book *Paris Plays* on Amazon and that you enjoyed reading it. I was delighted to hear that your drama group will be putting on one of the plays in the book this fall in Waterloo. You made my day.

In your email, you mentioned that you had read the review of *Paris Plays* in the *International Herald Tribune* and agreed with the reviewer who stated that I had a very good grasp on people in my writing. You asked me how one gets such a tool. You wondered if it were education or experience or a combination of the two. I can safely say that a person is not born with this ability. You must earn it. I will let you in on a secret on how I became a people person.

A person must get a handle on those around us to acquire patience. This trait must be earned as we are not born with it. It must be acquired and actually worked with in real life situations.

I had a good paying job at a high school in southern California at one time but I gave it all up to enter show business as a lifeline. I had several good prospects for earning money in show business and that encouraged me to give up my steady teaching paycheck. Unfortunately, as you might imagine all of the good possibilities faded as quickly as they had appeared. There I was without a paycheck and no prospect of getting one.

I was getting panicky when a teacher friend of mine offered to let me move in until I could get my life settled.

This friend suggested that I should apply for a job as a substitute teacher. I went to the local school district and applied. They hired me. This job then had me traveling to various schools all over the city to teach. Each day I had only a moment's notice to drive to the school and prepare some sort of lesson.

One day the principal at the middle school where I was subbing called me into his office. He asked if I had any experience teaching special education. I said no and stated that I hardly knew what the subject entailed. He said it was the opposite of gifted students and explained that they were not able to do ordinary curriculum work. He cut to the chase. A teacher had resigned and there was both a class of Spanish and a Special Ed U.S. History class that must be covered. He offered a steady income for the rest of the school year and delighted, I instantly agreed. One thing he wanted to know was if I had patience. I told him that I would try my best.

The next day I met with both classes for the first time. The Spanish class was like a dream of good students. Afterwards I went to the Special Ed US History class. There were 23 students and they looked at me as though I were from outer space. I guess they were expecting me to do something amazing. I didn't know what to do except jump in and act as though this were a rehearsal for a play.

I asked them who the first president was. Most answered that question correctly and I complimented them. I then had them to ask me questions which they did. One question was why my nose was so big. I told them it was because I could smell more than the average person. They seemed impressed. Then I took a book and read to them the poem *The Midnight Ride of Paul Revere*. I couldn't believe it, but they were absolutely quiet because I added a few sound effects. When I finished, they wanted me to read it again. Without hesitation I read it again and this time with even more gusto. Then I wrote about eight lines of the poem on the blackboard and we all read those together, making sound effects and whatever would bring life to the poem. The bell rang for them to go to their next class. They didn't want to go because they were having so much fun. That one hour with this class had taught me what patience is and its value in our lives.

US History, or my version of it, carried on day after day. When I arrived for the first class, the students were noisy and talked out loud to one another and paid very little attention to me. However, by the end of that first class I had them quieted down and following my lead. I had assigned them some questions. I asked Margaret why she had chewing gum on the tip of her nose. She patiently explained to me that in their math class it was the penalty for chewing gum in class. For some reason during that era one of the cardinal sins was to be caught chewing gum in class. I figured that if they wanted to chew gum we could have a chewing gum portion of the class, otherwise the rule stuck about wearing it on the tip of one's nose.

I gave them homework because they wanted to fit in like regular students. I handed out a couple of sheets of paper with states on them. They could color the different state and label them if they could. I always saw that homework consisted of two pages. That way those who did their homework got to use the stapler to staple it together. One day they were stapling when all of a sudden a student told me that Richard had taken the stapler and put it under his shirt. I didn't quiz him on why he had taken the stapler. I just mentioned that it would be known by others why stapling had stopped. This is what took patience.

One day a student came into class. She seemed disturbed and I asked her what was wrong. She told me that her stepfather gave her a quarter every time she slept with him. The previous night he had reneged and didn't give her the quarter. She wanted me to do something about it. I told her I thought she should go see the counselor. She did and we never saw her again. I was told she went into juvenile protection with a foster parent.

So it went and the steady paychecks kept coming in which were a blessing for me. Working with the Spanish students was no chore, and the class was quite responsive to learning the language. However, in my special education class things were of another world. I did develop great patience and it kept me on my toes to come up with things that would excite the minds which were a bit disadvantaged.

One day I was summoned to the principal's office. I wondered what I might have done that was considered incorrect. However, the principal complimented me and was very pleased and said the students had reported some very good things about me to their parents. Everyone was happy except Joyce, a young lady who taught the special education math classes. Joyce was at her wits end, mainly due to her lack of patience. The principal said that he thought it would be a good idea for us to swap classes. So, from that day on I taught math to special education students and Joyce taught US History.

So it went. Joyce seemed to be somewhat happier now that she wasn't trying to actually teach the special education kids math. I, on the other hand, just went into making up our own class money and playing bank account and store, etc. They could get an allowance of ten dollars and they would tell me what items they bought. This got them to see the concept of addition. I arranged for us to go to a bank as field trip outing. They were excited. The bank served punch and cookies and the students felt very special.

A couple of weeks after I took over teaching math, they wanted to know why we never talked about George Washington anymore. Thus went the rest of the year. The following year I got a full-time position teaching Spanish at a nearby high school.

One thing I know. Those special education students taught me patience and I saw the voice of humanity at work. We had a good time and met life at their level instead of trying to bring them up to my level. The big item I took away from this experience was to see people for who they are and not as they are supposed to be. So, when you read those plays of mine in *Paris Plays*, you can see how much Margaret, Richard and all of the others taught me so very much about the art of living.

Thanks again, David, for getting my book and do let me hear again once my play is in production with your drama group.

My very best to you,
Jack Fitzgerald

LETTER 13

LORRAINE

Dear Lorraine,

Thanks so much for your review of my play *Cold Duck*. I was glad that you enjoyed the play and that you especially liked the subtitle of "Cinderella According to Jack Fitzgerald." You stated in your review that you were intrigued that I would use this age old plot and be able to bring it up to nuclear-family standards.

Of all of my plays, this is my favorite. Since I was a child I have been fascinated by the *Cinderella* story. I guess most folks are. A down-and-out person is magically influenced by another person and in the process takes on another lifestyle completely.

The first version of this play was titled *Beautiful People* and was a more realistic, almost a soap opera version of the story. However, being that I had moved to Paris everything was kind of magical for me there. I decided to redo the entire play and make it real but with a great deal of fun involved.

When it came to writing the fairy godmother plot, I looked back over my experiences in life to see what I could or might use to have a modern-day fairy godmother.

After a good deal of thought, I remembered that one summer while living with my Aunt Ripple in Atlanta I applied to be a door-to-door encyclopedia salesman. I got the job but was told I must deliver a prepared speech to customers. I would tell them that their household had been chosen for a wonderful encyclopedia offer. I had a spiel with visual references on how great the set of encyclopedias were. The better the salesman was at giving the spiel, the better the chances were for a sale.

When rewriting the play and turning it into *Cold Duck*, I added a door-to-door saleslady character who is the "fairy godmother" in this modern setting.

Another character I added was a forlorn and disregarded daughter. Her mother was quite greedy and unkind to her. The mother had two more daughters who were attractive yet also unkind like her. They were leaving soon for a local fund-raising event to support an up and coming, handsome senator. The forlorn daughter, Erica, was again left at home. The door-to-door saleslady ("fairy godmother") arrives soon and magically transforms her into a princess. This quick transformation then places her in the company of the handsome senator.

Erica, the ersatz princess, doesn't have the expected glass slippers. Instead, the door-to-door sales lady, who represents Fashion Finery of Dallas and Beauty Bar Cosmetics of Kansas City, provides the magic that will transform the ordinary into the extraordinary. It turns out that her magic is some phony hip enhancers which will fill out Erica's lack of volume in that area. So, she loses these pads, not slippers, at the fundraiser and the prince (senator) chases her down to return them and finds his future bride.

I know I retold a lot, but I just wanted you to know how I came up with the plot. It was via my selling those encyclopedias in Atlanta. I do hope this provides you with a bit more inside information concerning *Cold Duck*.

Thanks again for the great review.
Jack

LETTER 14

KEN

Dear Ken,

Thanks for your recent email with memories of some of the times we have shared. Can you believe we are in our eighties? I can't. Eighty-nine for me, to be exact. I did appreciate the birthday card with the cute cat. Every time I think of you, it seems to have something to do with kitties, French, or cooking.

You asked me about my most memorable experiences from being in the US Army. I would have to say it was my 21-day trip on a troop ship from San Francisco to Yokohama, Japan.

I was in the Army and due to be sent overseas for two years to the Far East. My troop ship was leaving from San Francisco to Yokohama and the trip would be over Christmas and New Year's.

I had ten days leave to visit my folks in Okolona, Mississippi prior to leaving and then via train back to San Francisco. The troop ship was actually due to leave from a place called Camp Stoneman which was near San Francisco.

Due to train scheduling and special fare rates for the military I arrived three days earlier than planned at Camp Stoneman. The second day I was there the troop ship from Yokohama arrived and unloaded three thousand soldiers returning from overseas duty.

I found it exciting to hear all the stories of what was going to be my next couple of years, beginning with life on a troop ship called the *USS General Black*. The newly arrived soldiers were processed and sent to areas throughout the United States where they would be discharged.

I made a lot of friends while the people were waiting for their processing to be completed. I learned to play Blackjack and got pretty proficient at it. Several of the other Blackjack players gave me some quite useful information. They said the very first thing to do when you get aboard ship is not to lollygag around exploring the ship but instead run as fast as you can with your duffle bag to the sleeping quarters.

The sleeping area consisted of six layers of canvas tied to a rectangular pipe which was considered a bunk. My friends told me to hurry to this area and throw my bag up on the top rack so this would be my bunk. I thought the bottom would be better. They said absolutely not and that I would find out why if we ran into a tropical storm. They then told me the next thing I had to do after I threw my duffle bag on bunk number six was to run and try to find the Chaplin's office and see if you could talk to him. Fortunately, the Chaplin was in his office. My friends told me to beg him to let me work in the ship library. I told him I had all sorts of experience. I did as they instructed and soon found myself assigned to the library for the twenty-one day voyage of the *USS General Black* from Camp Stoneman to Yokohama.

I felt quite lucky to have made such friends who could tell me what I could do to make the voyage at least bearable as opposed to horrible.

The bunks filled up as there were three thousand soldiers who boarded the *USS Black* and we were to sail very late that afternoon. I was safely in the library playing Mr. Efficient. I had two associates who felt like they had escaped the guillotine too.

In the sleeping area I struggled that first night to crawl up to the sixth bunk and found it rather uncomfortable but managed to sleep. During the succeeding days I made friends with a guy named Wally from the bottom bunk. He had been assigned to work in the kitchen on the ship. He would relate how horrible it was to have to get inside the big cooking pots and scrub them clean after making spaghetti or some other similar sauce dish. He would return to his bunk and pass out.

About our tenth day aboard the *Black* we hit a typhoon and the *Black* bobbled around like a cork. That night in the bunks, many guys were seasick from the bobbing around in the Pacific. I thanked those Blackjack guys for warning me to get on that upper bunk. Poor Wally. It was like a Niagara Falls of vomit for him in bunk one.

The typhoon finally abated and poor Wally was in terrible shape. In those times, the classier magazines had beautiful ads for transatlantic liners. One such ad was for The French Line which had the headline, "Half the Fun Is in Getting There." Some person tore that out and put it on Wally's bunk. It was so ridiculous he himself was forced to laugh.

So here you have it, Ken, the story that combines something French with an Army experience of mine. Wally did survive and he became a good friend of mine for the rest of the time I was in the Army. I still have to thank those guys whose advice saved me from the certain drudgery of my getting to Japan.

Cheers,
Jack

General Black troop ship, 1953.

LETTER 15

RON

Dear Ron,

Not too long ago I was watching a performance of my play *FP One Forty* and my mind wandered back to a Christmas when you and Gary came to Paris to visit Ken and me. We were soon off on a Christmas and New Year's trip to visit our good friend Erwin in Stuttgart, Germany. We first went to the French Alps in southeastern France and visited Chamonix-Mont-Blanc. The four of us stayed in a very nice chalet and were snowed in for a couple of days. As it snowed outside, we built a fire and had a great time, probably one of my most memorable. You, Ken, and Gary all had the same high school English teacher in Morris, Oklahoma where you grew up. While I catnapped and you were busy writing postcards, Ken and Gary were busy diagraming sentences which they had learned to do in high school English. The competition was to see who could come up with the most difficult sentence to diagram and some got rather complex.

The snow let up in a couple of days and we were ready to get on the road to Zurich and later on to Stuttgart. Gary was very funny and he was a cornucopia of trivia and could tell such interesting stories. Remember as we drove through Switzerland, we smoked a pack of Fiesta cigarettes which we had picked up along the way. They were noted to be the most chic in the world. Their claim to fame was that the cigs were different pastel colors each with a gold filter. We laughed and laughed over these and, as the cabin of the car filled with dense smoke, we figured folks would think the car was on fire.

Gary was just downright clever in all his story telling and kept us in stitches. He told us about working at an employment agency in NYC for a while. People would come into the agency, obviously as dumb as stumps, and to get them ready to do even a menial job they would try to train them. He didn't work there very long.

You and Gary each bought beautiful overcoats in that fancy department store in Zurich. Because of our shopping we arrived late at Erwin's place in Stuttgart. Even so, it was instant fun because Erwin in his own way was like a German Gary. He spoke English very, very well and even taught it. He too had lots of stories about his father who was the commandant of a prison camp during WWII. He said as a kid he often wondered why their servants changed so often but did not know until much later that most of them had died in prison. That was not a fun story but he had a lot of other interesting stories and we heard him tell us how life was as a Hitler Youth.

After a couple of days with Erwin, we piled in the car and took off, the four of us, to visit friends of Erwin in Munich. Erwin had recommended that we stop at a small town not too far from Munich because there was a guy there who ran a Zarah Leander museums. You remember, Ron, you, Ken and I didn't have a clue as to who this person was. When we arrived at the private museum we were met by a very jolly, rotund man who guided us through his little museum. He explained that Leander was a Swedish film star, singer, and actress during the Hitler era and was the mistress of Goebbels, Hitler's propaganda minister. She was on the order of Hedy Lamar and her singing voice was rather lusty. One of her songs that was so good was entitled *Yes Sir*. It was a camp song about America's war effort being tied to the like of John Wayne etc. It was a catchy song and very interesting. Rudolph, the museum owner, played some film clips from several of her films made during World War II.

We left the museum and continued our trip to Munich where we hooked up with some friends of Erwin's, Ingobord and Deitlieb, and they showed us a marvelous time. Erwin told them that how impressed they were that we had visited the Zara Leander Museum. Like most gay Germans after the war, she had become one of their darlings. She continued singing into her nineties when unfortunately, she fell out of her wheelchair during a concert in Vienna and soon passed on to greater glory. As a farewell gift before we left to return to Stuttgart, Ingobord gave me an LP recording of Zara's most famous songs, which contained *Yes Sir*. I was delighted to get it.

I began thinking all these thoughts and going over old memories while watching a production of my play FP One Forty. Everyone in the audience was laughing and yet my mind was wandering. It wandered to our dear friend Gary, so talented but who only lived a couple more years because he was one of AIDS' first victims. We were all heart broken. So much of the stuff in this play FP One Forty had come directly from stories Gary had told me on that trip. And I had another play named *Yes Sir!* which was about show business and a drag queen that had a number to the song *Yes. Sir.*

Life is strange with its twists and turns and how rich it became for me by knowing people like you and everyone I have mentioned in this letter.

Very best to you.
Love, Jack

LETTER 16

TROY

Dear Troy,

I thoroughly enjoyed our dinner together the other night. I listened with interest to your story about how your father bought concert tickets in Los Angeles for an Elvis Presley concert. You told him you were not interested but he had already bought the tickets for you and your girlfriend. You said you weren't interested in such a concert, but you went ahead to please your father and girlfriend. You stated that you ended up liking the concert very much and was glad you went.

That is a nice little story with a beginning, middle, and end which all stories should have if they are to make a coherent statement of some kind.

I was going to launch into my Elvis story but decided not to because it doesn't have a beginning, a middle, and an end. I even have some doubt about writing about this to you. In writing one presents a group of facts and then connects the dots to form a story. My Elvis story presents dots, but no coherent story. Even though I decided I would write what I know as "My Elvis Story."

First of all, I must say that I will give you the facts, as I know them, but my problem is that I cannot connect them. Read on and you'll see what I am talking about.

My Elvis story has three locations: Okolona, the town I grew up in, Tupelo, Mississippi, nineteen miles north of Okolona, and the last location being Memphis, Tennessee.

Elvis was involved in all three locations. First, Elvis was born in Tupelo. If you drive through Tupelo you will see a shotgun house, long and narrow, which is listed as the birthplace of Elvis. Born in that house, his father Vernon Presley and mother Gladys Presley worked on the large farm of Alvis Corley from Okolona. Gladys was a housewife while Vernon was a sharecropper on the large farm of Alvis Corley.

Gladys gave birth to twin boys. During that era it was, and, I assume still is, the common practice of giving similar names to twins. Vernon, I figure in homage to Alvis Corley, named one twin Alvis and then the other Elvis, a made-up name based on Alvis. Little Alvis died and Elvis lived.

I am not sure what happened next in the life of Elvis. I know there have been dozens of books written about him, none of which I have read.

Here are some facts I do know. I went to Okolona Public School which was the first through the twelfth grades in one building. The bottom floor is the grammar school, the middle floor being the administrative offices and middle school, and the third floor being the high school.

I do know that Elvis had two first cousins who were called Big Red and Little Red Presley and they were the bullies of the playground and struck terror in my heart. They were not handsome but rather simian in features. I am older than Elvis so he also could have gone to Okolona Public School during grammar school. Then he went to live with his grandmother in Tupelo. Gladys had a brother, Dale Schumpert, who owned a furniture store in Okolona. He had a son named Butch Schumpert who looked very much like Elvis. He attended Okolona public schools until he graduated.

A complete blank dot goes in here because the next time I heard of Elvis, he was working in Okolona at the Stratford-Stratolounger factory.

My father worked for T and O Railroad his entire life. He managed the shipping department and coordinated shipments via rail boxcars from the Stratolounger factory to parts everywhere. So, my father knew Elvis quite well. He said he was a likeable person and loved hamburgers. My father said that Elvis remarked to him once that being rich to him meant he could eat all the hamburgers he wanted.

At that time Elvis and a friend of his, Charles Hankins, played and sang often at the Okolona Wilson Park Dance Pavilion. Then, after the Presley's moved to Memphis, comes a big blank dot in my recollection of Elvis and Charles.

That is the last I had heard of any of them in a long while. I left the Army in 1956 and returned from my station in Okinawa to attend Mississippi State University. One night while I was visiting my brother and his family, Paul remarked that on TV that night there was going to be someone from the local area perform. It was to be Elvis without Charles Hankins. I was thrilled. I thought he had done rather well but had no idea that he was already a hot ticket item.

Here the dots got all mixed up. I had no idea what has going on in the world of Elvis Presley. He just kept getting better known and famous and almost took on god-like status. He purchased lots of Cadillacs and a mansion in Memphis called Graceland. There he lived until he died.

I was vacationing on the island of Corfu off the Greek mainland. One evening while having coffee in a sidewalk cafe I noticed a newspaper being read by a customer next to me that had the headline, "Elvis Dead."

I couldn't believe that somebody from little Okolona and Tupelo could achieve such fame. Even so, this is an incomplete story. As I said at the beginning, there are dots to be connected but many dots are missing and the best I can say is that Elvis and my path in life was the same for a certain amount of time.

I generally keep from telling this as a story because it is just a bunch of facts which are unconnected. Anyway, I thought you might enjoy hearing about some of the early days in Okolona and Tupelo.

Very best to you. I hope you find this to be interesting.

Your friend, Jack

LETTER 17

ZEKE

Dear Zeke,

I just wanted to wish you a happy birthday. It is hard for me to believe that you are in your late twenties and married and out on your own with a fine job. It actually seems that you are two years old. When I would visit you and your mother you followed me around every place I went. If I got out of sight you would yell out "Uncle Jack, Uncle Jack." Then later on when you were a teenager you began asking me if I were your uncle. It was easier to say yes at the time and just avoid a long-winded explanation that still would bring up more questions than answers.

These days you are fully grown and for your birthday I thought I'd write you an email and tell you what I know about our relationship.

I think I told you about the rapid courtship and marriage of your great-great-grandmother, Lilian. Lilly was a tough French lady but was very pretty. Shortly after the marriage, she and her husband Prentis moved to Walla Walla, Washington. Lilly's first daughter, Ruth, was my mother and was born in Fulton, Mississippi. Lilly and Prentis lived with his parents in Fulton. Eventually Prentis took the family to the state of Washington to get into the lumber business. My mother, Ruth, was two years old at the time. Lilly became pregnant and had a second child, a daughter named

Ripple. Bad news, however, as Lilly suffered from uremic poisoning and was paralyzed on her right side for the rest of her life. The doctors in rural Washington said that she would never walk again. Lilly heard this and, being the tough person she was, she did manage to mention that she would indeed walk again one day. Lilly, Prentis, Ruth, and baby Ripple then moved back to Fulton, Mississippi, because Prentis's father was a doctor and could care for her. Lilly's strong will did actually get her up and walking with the use of a small chair to steady herself. She was paralyzed on the right side and dragged that foot when she walked, but she did walk and not only that, but she gave birth to three more children, and was an excellent cook.

Lilly's daughter Ripple was not her favorite child. I imagine it was because she associated her with her paralysis. Ripple on the other hand was a pretty, glamorous, and sprightly young lady. My mother said she was quite popular and before long she and a popular young man named Gordon were engaged. My grandmother disapproved because Gordon drank a lot and was a rounder. Ripple was intent on marrying him. Lilly told her that if she did, she was not welcome in their home anymore.

Ripple, being a headstrong person, went ahead and got married. Soon after their marriage Ripple became pregnant and had a daughter, which she named Dorothy.

Ripple was a go getter and worked to put herself and Gordon through college at Mississippi Normal in Hattiesburg, Mississippi. To Ripple's dismay Gordon remained a thorn in her sided mainly with his twin brother Sales who was also an alcoholic and a rounder. She soon figured out that she would have no future with such people, so she and Gordon divorced.

So, what to do with Dorothy? Lilly was not receptive to helping Ripple, so Ripple took Dorothy to live with my mother, Ruth. For my brother and me, Dorothy became our sister. Eventually though Lilly reunited and took Dorothy to live with her and Prentis in Fulton, where he was successful in the banking business. There Dorothy stayed until Prentis died.

Aunt Ripple was a businesswoman. She had taught school, then went into different businesses and ended up working in the early nineteen forties with a guy named Dale Carnegie and his niece to put out a book called *How To Win Friends and Influence People*. Aunt Ripple gave lectures and trained counselors which were sent everywhere. Dorothy was placed in a private girls school in Birmingham, Alabama. On holidays she would come to stay with us. I loved her visits because she and I could always find some fun things to do and sometimes she brought interesting friends on her visits to Okolona.

Dorothy never did like the name Dorothy so upon graduating from that young ladies school in Birmingham, she renamed herself Ripple Junior. Everybody in the family began calling her Junior. Junior eventual married and had two children, Rhett then Barbara. Junior's husband was killed in a car accident when Barbara was six weeks old.

Rhett, in his early twenties, was a boundless source of energy and held several different jobs ranging from disk jockey to running a telephone answering service. On one fateful night he was in an accident that left him paralyzed from the neck down. He did manage to hold on and live for nearly eighteen years in his condition with a great strength that rivaled his great-grandmother, Lilly. His sister Barbara attended university, majored in geology and worked in that area for several years.

Okay, Zeke. Barbara is your mother. Her mother Dorothy, aka Junior, was like my sister so, yes, I am your uncle.

I can tell how convoluted this all sounds and how it sounds like it would make some sort of novel, but I tried to give you a condensed version.

So, Happy Birthday,

Love,
Uncle Jack

PS. I always liked Aunt Ripple very much and she was always kind and generous to me. When I was eight years old she took me with her to Miami

Beach, Florida, where she was running a series of Carnegie seminars. We lived in a house owned by the Duke and Duchess of Windsor. Aunt Ripple bought me a suit and took me nightclubbing with her and her friends. I really lived that summer and Aunt Ripple was my kind of person. We remained close up to her death and I do miss her.

Ripple and Dorothy.

LETTER 18

RICHARD

Hi Richard,

Thanks so much for your letter telling me how much you enjoyed my book, *Contessa*. Yes, I do think it would make a great movie but so far no takers. I am very pleased though that you are going to recommend it to a friend of yours who is in the film business.

Also, I would like to comment on your statement about my ending up in Cuba and being there during and after the revolution. It was quite a stretch for me to go from Okolona, Mississippi, to Havana, Cuba into the middle of the Fidel Castro revolution of the late 1950s.

Most of the facts in my book *Contessa* are based on my actual experiences while living in Cuba. As I look back on my life, I too am amazed how some of these adventures unfolded.

Every story has to have a beginning. I graduated from Mississippi State University in May of 1958. My mother would attend the graduation, but my father couldn't because of work. However, a woman whom he had known for years worked at the railroad. She was like a fixture there and a very nice person to my father. My mother asked her to join us for my graduation ceremony as well as a celebratory tea being held at the home of the university president for students who were being honored for their work while at Mississippi State. I was a Presidential Scholar and thus my family and I were invited to the tea. Miss Olivia Murphey also attended and it seemed quite fitting. However, there was a bit of a tiff in the air due to a decision I had made just before leaving Okolona for Mississippi State that day. My mother was not very happy, because before we left Okolona, I had told her I was not going work locally but was going to go to Havana to live.

As mentioned before to many people, after graduating, the only work I could do with a degree in English was to teach school. The best job I could find was in another small Mississippi town called Clarksdale. They were paying the princely sum of $2,700 for the year. My mother thought it was a good deal although she would have preferred my getting a good job at the post office. No post office for me though. Miss Olivia, who was a sweet soul, tried to convince me that in the future salaries would go up and things could get better and for sure I would have a pension to count on.

However, a month or so before graduating, a Cuban living in my dormitory told me I could make more than that by teaching English in Havana. He wasn't from Havana and could not be of any help there because he came from the other end of the island, Santiago de Cuba. Anyway, he said that Havana would sure beat Clarksdale for liveliness. I decided to try it. I had a little money saved up from my time in the Army and that I would use it to get me started. My mother thought I had lost my mind. So, the elegant tea party after the graduation ceremonies was not all that happy an occasion.

My father thought it was a great idea and was all for me doing this adventure. Two weeks after the graduation and tea party, I boarded a Trailways bus in Okolona which took me to Jackson. From Jackson I got a Greyhound bus to Miami. I slept on the buses and wondered what in the world had I let myself in for by going off all by myself to a foreign country like Cuba. As the miles slipped by from Okolona and as I wheeled closer and closer to my destination, the more worried I became.

In Miami I could get a taste of Cuba because a lot of Cubans lived or visited there. I took a bus from Miami to Key West. This is a beautiful drive and goes from one little island to another island and finally ends up at Key West, which is the jumping off place for Havana. There were ferries to take you there for seven dollars or you could fly on Cuban Airways for ten dollars. I chose to fly. The night before I left, I like so many others went down to the dock area of Key West where people watch beautiful sunsets and enjoy the balmy weather. I knew I was no longer in Okolona and that the next day I would swap Okolona for Havana.

I took an early flight from Key West to Havana because I figured I needed the time to kind of set myself up in a hotel and see what was what in this very large city.

The plane landed at José Martí International Airport in Havana. José Martí was a big Cuban hero of the past. His grandson was Caesar Romero, the Hollywood film star. My first impression of Havana was in walking from the arrival room at the airport out to a bus that would take me to the central downtown area where it would deposit me for good, bad, or indifferent.

Cuba was something else. It had music in the air and the city was almost dancing with excitement. It was fun and exciting but scary to be there by myself.

I found a hotel very near where the bus let me out near the Malecon, the waterfront district. I got a room at a cheap hotel called the Packard but was being overcharged by the greedy woman who ran the place. She saw a pigeon.

That evening I took a stroll out on the Malecon, the port area where vendors of everything hawked their wares and where there were many sidewalk restaurants and bars. I went in a bar to have a beer, watch the passing parade, and think of how I was going to mix into living in this city. Out of nowhere an overly painted prostitute appeared and plopped herself at my table. She soon found out that I was not interested in her socially as her question, "Do you want some company?" drew a blank from me.

However, we did strike up a good conversation and she ended up buying me a beer. I told her why I had come to Havana and she was very impressed. She then told me about a movie she had seen that day, *La Violetera* with the Spanish film star Sarita Montiel. She said she could see it every day of the week. She then invited me to go see it the next day with her. We went and had a very good time watching the film and then having something to eat afterwards before she had to go to work. She then told me she would help me find a decent place to stay and a job teaching English. She became one of my best friends and true to her word, she got me set up in that capital city. All was just rocking along fabulously until the revolution hit and that transformed Cuba into another country under Fidel Castro. I remained there until I was deported as being an undesirable as were most Americans once the country turned socialist.

So, there you have the saga of how one goes from Okolona to Havana. There are good folks everywhere and life can be a giant hors d'oeuvre tray for sure. It has been for me.

Cheers and thanks again for your letter concerning my book, *Contessa*.

Your friend,
Jack

LETTER 19

JOYCE

Dear Joyce,

Thanks so much for the birthday card. I always appreciate receiving a card from you because you actually write a little newsy information on the inside of the card. I figure for the price of snail-mail one should get one's money's worth and use the white space inside the card to furnish some information. I know it was my birthday and it had nothing to do with your car troubles, but I was nevertheless interested in hearing about your plight. It is hard to believe that someone broke into your car and stole the battery. It certainly shows how vulnerable we are.

Your set of circumstances reminds me of two incidents in my life with cars that were just as troublesome. Cars are wonderful things when they work and don't produce headaches.

One time I was traveling from Mississippi State to visit a friend of mine in New Orleans. He was an Army buddy that I had not seen since we had been stationed together on the island of Okinawa, the location of fierce fighting and the last big battle of World War II. Anyway, I had just bought my first car, a 1949 Ford stick shift and of course it was a used car not a new one. I wanted to try it out and test it on a road trip, so I thought going to New Orleans to visit Sonny was just the ticket. As I traveled down the central part of Mississippi, I was nearing my destination. I had not driven in large traffic before and I was being extra cautious. I came to the bridge over Lake Pontchartrain and entered it. No more had I done so did I realize that I had not checked the gas gauge and saw it was almost on empty. I had not reckoned that the bridge would be over twenty miles long and that running out of gas would be a major disaster. To say I breathed heavy and hard would be putting it mildly. Every mile over that bridge was like a nightmare. I think I left the bridge with only fumes left in the gas tank. I had survived but the life lesson I learned that day was to always check the gas gauge and never let the tank get below one fourth full. I will say that in all my years of driving, I have always kept the tank with at least one-fourth full of gas. I never would want to go through that situation again.

I was in a second car situation that scared me. I had been home to Okolona to spend Christmas with my folks. After a week there, I got in my then car, a 1954 Chevrolet, which was a real wonderful used car. I cruised down through Mississippi toward Florida. I spent the night in Tallahassee and the next day would be a long day driving from the Florida State Capital to my home in West Palm Beach. I didn't like to drive at night but the last five miles would be through the Okefenokee Swamp, then civilization and then on to my apartment.

Night was coming on and I was truly in a wild area full of alligators, and you name it. All of a sudden my red light came on that signaled that my alternator was malfunctioning. There I was, right on the fringes of this terrible swamp and my car about to go kablooey on me. No civilization was near. I knew the car would conk out at any time. I was getting panicky just as darkness was falling. Hallelujah, out in all of that wildness appeared a service station. I just hoped my car would make it there.

Fortunately, it did. I pulled in and the place was closed. I didn't know what to do. I honked my horn and a light came on inside the back of the building. A man soon came to the front of the service station and yelled that he was closed. I told him in a loud voice that it was an emergency.

He told me to stay put and he'd be right out. It was very dark and the sounds of Mother Nature in the swamp were sounding very close to me. A friendly looking man came out and asked me what the problem was. I told him the alternator had gone out. He said he didn't have one and I asked him fearfully what was I to do. He said well if you stay where you are, the gators will probably get you. So, you 'd better get out of your car and come spend the night with us and tomorrow I'll go into West Palm Beach and get a rebuilt alternator for you. That is exactly what happened.

His wife was friendly and put me up on a cot in the back part of the service station. When I woke up the next morning, she was cooking breakfast. She said her husband, Willard, had already gone to get the alternator in West Palm Beach and would probably be back soon if he found a rebuilt one.

Things worked out just fine. Willard arrived and we all had breakfast together. His wife ran the filling station part of their business. She pumped gas and gave out information. While I tried to be of help, Willard installed the new alternator and before long I was on my way to West Palm Beach and to resume my duties as a Spanish teacher at Riviera Beach High School.

This was far too much to write to you on a Christmas card or your birthday card, so I will send it to you in an email. Thanks again for getting in touch. I will end this email by saying that life can be very interesting, and we have to expect the unexpected.

Thanks again for the neat birthday card.

Love, Jack

LETTER 20

DAN

Dear Dan,

Thanks so much for your birthday greeting and phone call. Talk about long friendships, ours is a case in point. Just to think, I taught you Spanish when you were a junior in high school which means we have kept up with one another for over fifty years. Well, that is not exactly correct. I taught you Spanish in high school in Riverside, California, when you were about sixteen or seventeen years old. After that year I went to teach Spanish at New York State University in Plattsburgh. Then a big skip in time. I left Riverside for Plattsburgh, then to Paris, France and finally back to California.

One fine day in 2000 or so, a friend of mine and I were having breakfast at the Silver Spoon Café in West Hollywood. We had come in from Palm Springs where I was then living. While enjoying my omelet a voice from the next table asked me if I were Mr. Fitzgerald, a former Spanish teacher. I looked up and there you were. I recognized you immediately and my first thought was what happened to that full head of hair you used to have? We rekindled our knowledge of one another.

You said you had attended the Air Force Academy and were now out of the Air Force. You told me you worked with computer programming. You asked if I had a website, and I barely knew what a website was. You then offered to build a free website for me since I had been such a memorable teacher. You lived in Riverside, not far from Palm Springs, and in short time you had built my website at jackfitzgerald.com. Together we also managed to set up a blog covering my writings and many other things. And we've been working together on various projects until my recent 89th birthday. You have been of invaluable help to me in my creative efforts and as a wonderful friend.

I remember you once asked me how it was that a southerner from Okolona, Mississippi, could become a Spanish teacher not only on the high school level but at the university level. I always planned to tell you how that came to be, but somehow other things got in the way and I never got around to answering that question. So, I just decided that on my 89th birthday I was not so pressured for time that for certain here was the moment to come clean on that particular question.

You didn't know my father but be assured that Spanish being a part of my life was his doing. He was a very smart man but due to various circumstances he was never formally educated past the eighth grade.

When he was fifteen, he went to work full-time for the railroad. He did not have the resources nor time to pursue a formal education so he actually became self-educated. He read every book he could get his hands on and worked hard to become very learned on many subjects. My father decided that when he married he wanted children. He soon met Ruth, my mother, and they eventually had two sons, Paul and me. Our first cousin, Dorothy, lived with us and was like our sister.

He enrolled in a mail order Spanish course offered by the Cortina Academy. He listened to all their records and memorized all of the phrases. With Dorothy living with us, she became his first effort at teaching a foreign language to another. Everything he said to her was in Spanish and was the same with my brother Paul and me. Our mother went along with it all but not with great enthusiasm and vowed not to take part in his experiment. Dorothy and Paul had good success, but I was stubborn. I would only do things which he told me to do in Spanish but would not speak back to him. And so it went. I was not really a success in the experiment.

My father only spoke to us in Spanish or in his brand of Spanish that he had learned via those phonograph recordings. After my first year at Mississippi State, one of my Spanish professors told me about a course for foreigners at the University of Mexico in Mexico City. Suddenly it occurred to me that this might be a way for me to get away from Mississippi for a spell. So, I played up to my father in Spanish and he got me a pass on a train heading to Mexico City. The train left Laredo, Texas on the Aztec Eagle, a very nice train. My mother was not for me going there by myself but my father was all for it. So, this intrepid little Okolonian was on my way to Mexico City. At the time I was only 19 years old.

During the very crowded train ride I sat with a Mexican family consisting of a grandmother, grandfather, a young teenage granddaughter, and me. They shared their food with me and we became quite friendly. As best I could I used the Spanish I had learned from my father. Every time I said something in Spanish, the grandmother would laugh. Finally, I asked the young girl why her grandmother was laughing. She said it was because I sounded like a recording. I realized that all those phrases my father learned from Cortina Academy were very pedantic and definitely not life like.

Anyway, I went to the special courses at the University of Mexico and then later for a year to Mexico City College, a specialized school for Americans studying Spanish. The first trip to Mexico was before I went into the Army and the Mexico City College portion was as far as I got. Once out of the Army my education was paid for by the G. I. Bill of Rights. I returned to Mississippi State for my last year and majored in English with a minor in Spanish. From there I went to live in Cuba until I was pitched out on my ear by the rebels after the revolution in the late fifties. I then went to Middlebury College on a Spanish Government Scholarship and attended the University of Madrid for a year and where I received my master's degree.

I then returned to the America where I taught Spanish at Wake Forest University, several high schools, and then abandoned Spanish all together and moved to Paris, France where I lived for ten years.

So, there you have it, my good friend, Dan. That is how one becomes a Spanish teacher via Okolona, Mississippi or at least this Spanish teacher.

Cheers and very best to you. And thanks for all your help.

As always,
Jack

LETTER 21

TOM

Dear Tom,

Thanks for your birthday greeting. I was glad that Ricardo had such a good time on your recent trip. You mentioned that Ricardo had just finished reading my book *Contessa* and wanted to know if the parts in it concerning habu were indeed correct or just my vivid imagination at work.

Please tell Ricardo that I can safely say that everything written about the habu in *Contessa* was based on actual events that occurred to me while I was in the Army serving overseas. I will go into some details here that were used as the basis for plot points in my book.

In 1953 I joined the Army. I must admit that at the time I was having a hard time surviving and the Army seemed to be the perfect way to get three meals a day and have a place to sleep. Besides, I opined that I would get the G.I. Bill of Rights once I got out and it would pay for my education. How could I lose, I thought?

So, into the Army I went. I had basic training at Camp Breckinridge, Kentucky, then on to Fort Devens in Massachusetts for three months of training for service in the intelligence corps known as the Army Security Agency. I learned a lot during those three months about the art of intelligence and I have been able to use that training in my writing, mainly my two murder mystery novels, *Teddy Bear Murders*, and, *Murder Impossible*. The time came for my deployment and I was hoping I would be sent to Germany so that I could have a couple of years of European living. However, that did not happen. I was put on a troop ship headed for Yokohama, Japan, where I was sent to my final destination, that being Okinawa. I knew two things about Okinawa. It was the last big battle of World War II in the Pacific where many people were killed on both sides of the war. The other thing I knew about Okinawa was that it was the site where my sister Dorothy's fiancée, a pilot, was shot down and killed. So, my going there did not set well with her at all.

A couple of days after being informed of our orders, I was waiting for a ship to take me from Yokohama to Okinawa, an island 57 miles long and seven miles wide. While waiting in line to board the ship, we had to wait for some returning soldiers to get off the ship. I was curious to know what the place was like so I asked one of the returning soldiers who had spent a year and a half there, what it was like. He mentioned that there was very little to do as most things had been destroyed in the war. But beware of the habu, he stated, with a look of trepidation on his face.

"Habu?" I asked, "What is that?" I was then told it was a large cobra native to that island and they were everywhere. They were super poisonous and nasty. I, who hated snakes, felt a big lump in my chest. I was slated for two years on that island and now, not only did I have to fight being in a strange place, I had to watch out for a certain species of cobra. He said that the week before some GIs were riding in a truck that went off the road and pinned seven soldiers down in the jungle. They were bitten by habus and all died. He added that Okinawa had typhoons and that is when habus looked for shelter and you really had to be careful.

I landed in Okinawa. It was already a foreboding place to me due to the fact that Dorothy's fiancée had died there and I was going to have to fight the battle of the habus.

There was very little to do in Okinawa. Every so often the natives put on habu-mongoose fights. The mongoose always won so everyone felt okay and applauded.

Things went fine for my first year there. I did see a couple of habus on their own looking for someone to bite, I would imagine. Then I made corporal in rank and with this came the possibility of living off base if I wanted. Generally, this meant that a soldier tied up with a native honey and they rented a little cottage and set up housekeeping. I was not interested in any of that but what I was interested in was getting off base on my three days off each week. I went to a nearby village and spoke to Pappa San, the mayor who was also the local real estate agent. He set me up in a quaint little straw thatched cottage. I bought a few things to make it seem homey. I even wrote my father that I had a place for a garden, and he sent me some seeds to plant. I started digging to plant some carrots, etc. but in kept finding skulls in helmets and other things left over from the war. So that was that with the garden.

I thought that I would try to make a movie with a recently purchased 8mm Riviera camera. I got a team of others and we turned the little cottage into our studio to try to make a film and use a tape recorder for some music and sound. We dubbed our little studio Morgue Studios due to the items lurking in the ground near the cottage. So far, I had not spent the night in the cottage but with some friends, we thought we would test it out. To our amazement, once things got quiet, big rats that lived in the thatched area of the roof scurried across the ceiling planks and kept us up all night. The next morning, we saw that they had almost destroyed our little kitchen and studio. I reported this to Pappa San and he smiled and told me there was a cure. He said he would fix it. The next night we tried staying there. Everything was quite peaceful. I complimented Papa San for fixing the problem. He said he had put a habu in the ceiling of the cottage and the rats quickly left. I told him there was no way I would stay in the place knowing that a habu was sharing it. He said that I should then buy a mongoose from him which he raised and sold. So, I bought a mongoose and so things worked out just fine. No rats as they were scared of the habu. No habu as it was scared of the mongoose. The mongoose is not really a tame little animal, so it has to remain in its cage. Even so, as I look back on things now, I can't believe I slept in a place with a live cobra afoot.

One night I left the cottage to go back to camp for a late shift of work and I went to the area near where Papa San lived and waited for a rickety bus that came by every so often and would take me back to camp. I smoked at that time and always while waiting, I would smoke a cigarette. So, I was puffing away and waiting for the bus. Out of my eye I caught what I thought was a leaf floating in the air, but it didn't land. As I moved my lighted cigarette, the leaf moved. Then it hit me. That was no leaf. It was a habu fully upright and it was being hypnotized by the light of my cigarette. I almost fell over but got near enough to Papa San's house to shout out in a whisper voice, "Habu!, habu!, habu!." I was hoping Papa San would hear me. After doing this and hoping my cigarette lasted, the door to Papa San's house opened and out scurried a mongoose. It jumped onto the cobra and killed it very quickly. The lumbering native bus arrived, and I got on it and went back to camp and decided not to be out after dark again.

As to our little film project. We did make it and showed it in the recreation room with all sorts of fanfare. What people won't do to kill time.

So, there, you can let Ricardo know these are the real facts that served me well in my book, *Contessa*.

Thanks again for the birthday wishes,
Cheers, Jack

Morgue Studios.

Photo of a habu. (Shawn M. Miller, 2014©)

LETTER 22

ABBY

Dear Abby,

Thanks for your telephone call wishing me a happy birthday. It is hard for me to believe that you still live in Paris. You and I taught English as a foreign language at a private language school there in the seventies.

I left to go to Hollywood and work on a screenplay I had written. You remained in Paris and I guess that makes it about forty years that you have been there and we have managed to keep in contact. I know when we talked on the phone last you were interested in my novel writing, thinking that maybe you might like to give it a try. You wanted to know how I came up with the books I have written and how they were been published.

As I told you on the phone there is no short answer to that question. Maybe I will have more success with this email. My answer may be a little disjointed but at least it will be an answer to your question.

First of all, when he was about fourteen, my older brother asked me what I wanted to be when I grew up. Kids always ask one another that question. I told him I wanted to be a writer. He smirked and said that if I were going to write, I'd first have to live and so far I hadn't lived. His words did strike at my psyche and I knew he was in a way somewhat correct. However, he was discounting that we lived in Okolona, Mississippi, and that such small Southern towns are just hotbeds for plots of all sorts. After all, Okolona's population was only a mere 2,000 but we could really hatch some stories from living in such a small town. I reckoned that this little town was unique in that it had a full dozen old maid sisters living together. We called ourselves the little city that does big things. There was lots of intrigue and gossip going on with those dozen old maids and since I was a gregarious youth, I visited most of these maiden ladies and heard a lot of their stories. And to think, Paul believed I had nothing to write about.

I did realize that my brother was talking about life outside of Okolona. Over the years I did have lots and lots of adventures and remembered the stories of a lot of these old maid sisters. There were Aunt Liza and her sister Aunt Sally and both had been slaves when they were very young. They were the ones who told me you could buy and sell people. I couldn't believe that and certainly needed to check that out at the local library.

So, let's jump to my adulthood, say about age thirty-five. I was involved in an accident which caused me to have a broken kneecap. I was operated on and a pin was put in. I had a cast on my leg up to my thigh which confined me to a wheelchair for six weeks. Then the cast came off and I had physical therapy to learn how to walk again. It looked like I was going to be housebound for at least three months. I, of course, was on leave from my position as a Spanish teacher at the local high school in the town where I lived in California and felt trapped with nothing to do.

One day I read an article that Margaret Mitchell, the author of *Gone with the Wind*, had been laid up with an accident. She read books from the library but her husband soon tired of fetching them for her and suggested instead that she write a book. That is what she did. She wrote and wrote and out came *Gone with the Wind*. Her main character was Pansy O'Hara but eventually a publisher said she had to change that name. Margaret had a red cocker spaniel and so she named the character Scarlett O'Hara. The rest is history. Margaret, though, never wrote another book.

There I was laid up with nothing to do. I decided that I would write a book. I had no plot in mind, I had no central character, nor I did know how to write a novel. Even so, I picked out the name of my main character and used Olivia from Miss Olivia who had worked at the railroad with me. She and her maiden sister, Miss Ida, were interesting types so I used the name Olivia and patterned her after Miss Olivia.

It took me about three months to write the book. I worked on it every day. Once it was finished and I was once again mobile and back on my job at the high school, I thought I would see if I could sell the novel. I contacted agents in New York and out of all the answers got one agent who worked with me on the novel. She wasn't really excited about it because it was rather turgid, and Olivia wasn't an exciting main character. I did some rewrites and eventually put the manuscript in a drawer and forgot about it and got on with my life.

Jump forward another thirty-five years and in that time, I had learned to write, was making a living at it, and had a voice in my writing. Voice is how the person tells the story via humor, facts, turgidly, you name it. My original novel had been called *Teddy Bears Get Tired* and it was about Olivia, a schoolteacher who was tired of being on the short end of the stick in life. That part got the attention of an agent in New York, but she said I had no voice. However, after those thirty-five years I had developed a voice in my writing and as a lot of people told me, my writing sounded just like I was talking to them. They could visualize me. That manuscript really inhabited a lot of drawers over those thirty-five years.

One day I was gathering together my writing into some semblance of organization, and I ran across my novel about Olivia. I looked over it and could see how and why it never got published. It wasn't good and for sure had no voice. I thought that as a project I might rewrite the thing and see what I could make out of it. Olivia became a Miss Marple sort of amateur sleuth who was a high school English teacher. There was a murderer a foot in the high school and Olivia's sleuthing told her that she was probably slated as the next victim. The murderer would leave a teddy bear at the scene of each murder. The name was changed to *Teddy Bear Murders* and was published in short order. It did have a voice and one can actually see Olivia via her voice and actions.

So, Abby, that is how I see writing. You have to write about that which you know and make it live on the page. Write for readability which means use very few three or more syllable words, short sentences of sixteen words or less, and paragraphs of about four to six sentences. Add color by using colorful words. Instead of saying "she said," write "she screamed."

So, there you have not only some tricks of the trade but some encouragement to go get started on your own book. One warning though, writing a book takes a lot of work and on a daily basis. Most book projects never get past the second chapter because that is when the would-be author sees the hard work ahead, and thus quits.

Take care, and so glad we are still in contact.
Cheers, Jack

Taking in the sites of Paris.

Jack in Paris.

Eiffel Tower.

LETTER 23

BRENDA

Dear Brenda,

Thanks for the lift to Ellen's party last week. I think we all had a great time, and she really knows how to throw a fun get together. When you came to my apartment, I invited you in because I wasn't fully ready to go. Once all systems were on go, I reappeared and told you I was ready to go party. You walked over to the wall and pointed to an art item there. You remarked that this was a Russian icon of the sixteenth century. The background was wood with alabaster on it, you remarked, and that the nativity scene was painted on it. I was surprised that you knew this much about Russian artwork, especially peasant art icons. You smiled and said that you had not wasted your time in your art class in college. You asked me how I came to acquire this particular piece of artwork and I replied that I would let you know another time because if I told you the whole story, we would be late for Ellen's party.

You said that being Ellen's secretary, you knew it would not do to arrive late. I agreed but promised you I would give you all the details about my iconic artwork at a later time. I thought I might have time at the party, but I didn't. Ellen, Dean of Woodbury University's graduate division, had invited her faculty and we did have a lot to chit-chat about. I taught Communications and Theatre at Woodbury for several years.

Anyway, Brenda, there is no time like the present. I decided I'd just write you about that icon via email because I don't know when another occasion together would come about.

So, here is the skinny on my having that beautiful icon hanging on my wall. After I finished my year of study at the University of Madrid and received my master's degree, I ran into a YMCA group who was on a ten-day trip to the Soviet Union. I knew one of the members and asked if I might join in with the group. I was accepted and after I finished up at the University of Madrid, I was on my way to Helsinki, Finland where our tour would begin.

While in the Finnish capital for two days before the trip, I noticed others were buying ball point pens, chewing gum, socks, and other miscellaneous things. I assumed that they were getting these items to hand out to Russians they met. That was half of the answer. Their real plan was to swap these items for cash or artwork on the Soviet black market.

I must explain something. In the early sixties the Soviet Union was not really open to the West. We were there due to the YMCA. I was told that in Russia they were unsure as to even what simple chewing gum was and that ball point pens were worth a lot as well as being super valuable. Items like radios, class rings and all things with an American touch were highly valued. The morning before our train left, I ran quickly to the nearest Finnish department store and bough chewing gum, ball point pens and several pairs of socks.

We first went to St. Petersburg, formerly Leningrad. We stayed there several days and were told not to pay attention to the black market people milling around and selling items. Things they sold could not give you items in return that were of much value. My fellow travelers were waiting for Moscow. I was glad I listened to them. I saw firsthand that life was really dismal in most of the Soviet Union and that they had few luxuries in their life. People were friendly but most were not engaging due to everything around them being drab, drab, drab. Once our very sweet tour guide, Vera, told us that the factory we were going to visit had recently won the Lenin Prize for Manufacturing. A guy from California in the back of the bus shouted out, "One more prize and they can get a stick of gum." Everyone laughed. Even Vera. Chewing gum was a mystery to them. It was part magic because you could chew it forever and it never broke up.

We stayed at the Hotel Metropol Moscow which is described as luxurious but my interpretation is that it is a rather dismal fortress with few comforts. One thing we all got a kick out of was that the toilet paper was more like waxed paper and not pleasurable to use.

The center of nighttime activity was in Red Square in front of Lenin's Tomb. We had visited this place and it contained not only Lenin but also Stalin. They both looked very alive in their glass coffins. Very eerie.

At night the black market thrived. I, like so many other fellow travelers, soon got rid of the ball point pens, chewing gum and socks traded for small art items which apparently had been looted from churches and monasteries during the revolution. What these black-market people really wanted was electronics such as a transistor radio. I tried to find out if the police were able to arrest people for these black market activities. I was told in principle yes but more than likely the people they were dealing with were the police who wanted first dibs on any possible loot.

I had not bought a lot of items to sell so I soon ran out. I was talking with a very friendly man one evening and told him I had nothing more to swap. He seemed disappointed. He was very nice and invited me home with him for dinner. His name was Youri and his entire family lived in one apartment, including grandparents. The toilet was right next to the stove where dinner was being prepared. I, unfortunately, had to use the bathroom and told him. He showed me to the commode in the kitchen. Nobody seemed to care as I took a seat and attended to business. I was just so glad that I lived in a country with better arrangements.

After dinner, Youri and I chatted and drank some vodka. He wanted to know if I had perhaps a radio or something like that. I told him I had a very nice General Electric portable short-wave radio. Well, bingo! This was exactly what he was looking for. Then he told me he would give me an icon and five hundred French Francs for my GE radio. I agreed. We went to the Metropole where I picked up the radio and then we went to police headquarters which scared me to death. It turned out Youri was a cop, and we went there so he could get me the icon and my francs. He then escorted me back to my hotel and we parted on very pleasant terms.

I didn't tell anybody about what had happened. The icon was sixteenth century folk art, and I really did not know what to do with it. Anyway, I kept my icon hidden. The day we left Moscow to return to Finland, I wore a jacket and put the icon in the back of my shirt and jacket. Things went just fine until we hit Vibor, Russia, which is at the border with Finland. We had two hours there before the train would be allowed to leave Russia. I walked around and at one point sat and had a cold treat, sort of a Popsicle. The train whistled that it was time to board. I got on and found a seat where I could sit upright. I was ready to get out of Russia as fast as we could. I was told to get out my passport for a check. Unfortunately, my search for it came up negative. No passport. I had lost my passport. There I sat with that icon in my back and no passport. I had no alternative but to tell the head of the tour that I had lost my passport. He said that it was terrible, but he would see what he could do. Soon there was an announcement from inside the train station that said a lot of things in Russian that I could not understand. Shortly thereafter, everybody in and outside the train began searching for my passport. The good news is that an older lady found it under the bench where I had stopped to have that Popsicle. I gave her a ball point pen, my last one, and quickly boarded the train.

That night at our hotel in Helsinki everyone came clean on what they had gotten from their trip to the Soviet Union. It looked like an art show.

Anyway, I did end up taking that icon home to Okolona where it stayed until my parent's death some years later. And here it is now on the wall of my present-day apartment. It is a beautiful thing and does have a story behind it. If it is from the 1600's then think of all the stories and history it has been around. So, there you have the story behind the painting.

Very best to you.
Cheers, Jack

LETTER 24

HERB

Dear Herb,

It was so good to see you and John at a performance of my play *News From Freida* in the theater at Woodbury University in Burbank. I enjoyed our chat after the play and would like to have spent more time with both of you but the cast of the play had an event that I had to attend. I did, though, want to expand on John's question about the origin of this play. He said he thought it was very unusual and wondered how I came up with the basic premise of the play.

I figured that an email would have to do and be a much quicker answer. I believe you and John enjoyed the production so much that you said you were going to see it again and bring friends next time around.

Okay, here is the skinny on *News From Freida*. As you could tell, the play is not divided into acts but sketches. There are twelve of them.

My very first produced play in Paris, where I was living at the time, was called *Killing Time*. It had an unusual history, but I have already told you about that in previous get-togethers. It was successful, I was glad to report. One night after a performance of *Killing Time*, a rather imposing French gentleman sought me out. He introduced himself to me as the owner of a very nice café theatre in Paris called The

Harlequin Parnas. He told me the place consisted of an upstairs stage and a downstairs stage. He remarked that he had a play he was doing at the moment occupying the top floor stage. He said a theater group had intended putting on a play in the basement theater but that they had suddenly cancelled. He mentioned that he was looking for a replacement and asked me if I had a play available. I did not have a play. The only play I had was *Killing Time* and it was being produced at the moment in a rather dowdy theatre.

I did not know what to do. Here was an opportunity to further my career as a writer but I had nothing. Even so, I said, with the straightest of faces, that I did indeed have a play. He was quite pleased and said that the arrangement was that he and I would split the money from ticket sales. The kicker was that my play had to come off in two weeks. I was terrified. This man was rather unfriendly by nature but at the time I didn't care. We shook hands on the deal, and we left. I asked him no questions and he asked me none. The idea was that we would open in two weeks.

I got back to my apartment and wondered what had I done. It is practically impossible to rehearse a play after finding actors in a two-week frame but even worse if you have no play for them to rehearse. I had no idea what to do. I contemplated calling him on the phone and telling him that I too had to pull out of the commitment. I just didn't know how I would approach it and I knew that if I did not keep up my end of the bargain I would not have this opportunity again.

Nervously, I looked though my mail and there was a letter from my father's first cousin, Sally Kelly, who was a poet and short story writer. In her yearly newsletter she told about all the things she and her family had done that year. I smiled because most people who got her newsletter said they would really like to know what the unvarnished truth was. All of a sudden it hit me. Why not take her newsletter and adapt it as a series of twelve sketches. An actress would orally tell you the newsletter and then four actors on stage would show you what really happened. I got busy that very moment at my typewriter. I could not use Sally's name because I didn't know if she would be complimented or angry with me. Instead, I used Freida as the name of the newsletter sender. Freida was the name of a South African friend and fellow teacher where I taught. So, I typed out the title, *News From Freida.*

I hastily wrote the sketches for January, February, and March. The play would begin with an actress portraying Freida to come down the stairs into the basement theater and say to the audience "Hi, it's Freida. I'm sorry, but I'm going to have to do it to you once again and send you my yearly newsletter, otherwise I'd never be able to fill you in on all the things that happened to my family on a Christmas card. Well, let's see. Where to begin."

She then tells some marvelous things that she, her husband Mac, and son and daughter did in January of the past year. That faded into the characters on stage acting out what really happened.

The next day I put an ad for actors in the *International Herald Tribune.* I was amazed at the good talent I got, especially the actress who played Frieda. She was a Broadway and film actress and really knew her stuff. She turned Freida into a total delight. The play did indeed open in two weeks. It was an instant crowd pleaser and became so popular that a second cast had to open at the theatre on alternate days.

The owner of the theatre turned out to be one tough person to work with. He had the beautiful upstairs stage, and he was lucky to have half a dozen people attend. He starred in a one-man show called *The Man Who Vomited Rabbits.* No wonder so few people attended. On one hand he loved all the money Freida was raking in and was jealous because his vomiting rabbit show was a miserable flop. He was terrible to work for but we persevered and the success of *News From Freida* in Paris opened up the possibility for a three act play of mine to be produced at the famed Le théâtre du Tertre, the site where the Can Can was invented and displayed.

So, there you have it. So many times in life I have found that we let fate make our decisions for us. What if Sally had not sent me that newsletter at that very particular moment in time? Anyway, she did and the rest is history. Enjoy your second viewing of *Frieda* with your friends.

My very best to both of you,
Jack

LETTER 25

BUZZ

Dear Buzz,

Thanks for inviting me out for lunch the other day to my favorite restaurant here in Palm Springs. One thing I can say for sure is that we are never at a loss for conversation. I must admit I love every bit of it as my mind seems to operate the same way.... always searching for new and interesting topics to cover while having good food and wine.

Unfortunately, sometimes we get on one topic and it turns into another topic and we never do cover the original topic. I am afraid that is what happened the other day when you were asking me about my life in Mexico. You said that you had considered living there once upon a time but never did get up the nerve to give it a try. I was about to launch into providing information on that topic when, before we knew it, we were talking about the south of France and your upcoming trip there.

Allow me to use this email to tell you about my experiences living in Mexico. The first time I was just nineteen and had finished my first year at Mississippi State University. The second time was after I got out of the Army and I had attended Mexico City College. The third time was in the nineteen-nineties when I was working on a screenplay in Acapulco and truly living first class.

So, the first time to Mexico was in 1951. My father, who worked for the railroad, got me a free ticket on The Aztec Eagle train from Laredo to Mexico City, a very long journey. My mother was one hundred percent against my going way off to a foreign country all by myself. I did speak some Spanish, thanks to my father and his self-taught home study course via The Cortina Academy. The train trip was very exciting and I loved every minute of it. However, as we neared the capital, I could tell it was an immense city. It suddenly struck me that I would get off of the train in Mexico City and then what? I didn't even have much information concerning the Center for Studying English via the University of Mexico. My mother was correct. What in the world was I doing in such an out-of-the-way place and for what good reason? I didn't have very much money and I had no idea what to do.

The train station was immense and overflowing with people. A tourist was looked upon as a source of money and so I was pounced on by every taxi driver there plus every guide.

I was terrified. I had to fight people off from taking my luggage. I saw a policeman and ran over to him. He had a badge that said Turista. That meant, I presumed, that he was to help people like me. He didn't speak much English in spite of his lofty position but he could tell that I was in deep trouble.

He told me to come with him. He put me in a police car and took me to some part of what he called downtown Mexico City, near the gigantic monument to the revolution of 1910. He took me inside a small, clean hotel called the New York Hotel.

At that time for one dollar you got eight and a half pesos. I had not exchanged my money yet, so I had no pesos. The hotel obviously gave the Turista policeman a cut for bringing me there and the price for the hotel was seven dollars a night. In the early fifties, believe it or not, that was thought of as extravagant. To show you that it was expensive, I had fifty dollars in all for this Mexican adventure. I could see I wouldn't last a week there. I decided to spend one night there and then the next day see if I really should just tuck tail and return home to Mississippi. The room was nice but I knew I was being taken. Once they added extras into the charges, it was going to cost me ten dollars a night.

The next morning, I got up and left the hotel for a bit to see where in the world I had been parked. It all looked very interesting, but I had no idea what to do or where to go. I went into a small restaurant on the park square nearby and ordered breakfast. I told the woman I wanted jabon y huevos fritos. She laughed and I just took it that my Spanish sounded strange to her. Anyway, soon she came back with a plate. It had a bar of soap on it with two fried eggs. They were laughing.

A very jolly woman came in for a quick visit and got in on the joke and laughed. I looked at the plate and knew immediately why they were laughing. The word for ham in Spanish is jamon and the word for soap is jabon. I had merely mispronounced it. Anyway, the woman brought me a plate with a nice portion of fried ham. The waitress left.

Her friend came over with a big smile on her face and told me her name was Charley and asked me my name. Her English was very good and she was in her early fifties. She then took a seat and told me she liked interesting people and that I looked like an interesting person to her. Somehow I felt at home with this woman and told her all about coming from Mississippi to study Spanish at the school operated by the University of Mexico. I asked her if she knew the place and she said no. She asked me where I was staying, and I said the New York Hotel. She frowned and told me to hurry and finish my breakfast. I wondered why we were in a hurry, and she told me that she was moving me out of that gyp joint and putting me up in the house where she lived and worked as a maid. She told me it was nice and they would make me a special price of fifty pesos a week which was only about six dollars for the week.

It turned out that Charley lived just off the park in a very nice home and a museum operated by the wife of the famous Mexican painter, Diego

Rivera. She said the senora rented a few rooms to supplement her private museum there. Well, the senora turned out to be really kind of bitchy, but everyone loved Charley. She moved my stuff to a great room there. Then two days later she appeared at my room and was dressed like the Queen of Sheba. She told me that we were going to that school and see if it was legit. She said she had to dress up to impress the people.

Charley not only found the place but got me registered in three classes there and told the teachers that she hoped they could improve my accent. I went to school there for three months and lived in that very nice home and really met some interesting people. Charley even got me a part time job every so often as an extra in Mexican films. They had to have Caucasian types in nightclub scenes and the like. So, this trip lasted three months and was great fun. Charley may have only been a maid, but she ran everyone's life for them, even Diego Rivera whom she thought was terrific. When I was returning to the states, Charley threw a large fiesta for me with music and lots of good food. Charley was one of the most memorable people in my life.

So there you have it, Buzz. Those other times in Mexico will have to wait for another lunch at our favorite restaurant.

Cheers,
Jack

Paul, Jack, and dad.

LETTER 26

ELAINE

Dear Elaine,

I wanted to write a note of appreciation to you for suggesting three of my books for your book club. I really enjoyed meeting with your fellow members and discussing my book *Viva La Evolución*. The question-and-answer periods of these meetings are always a lot of fun for me and it appears for the readers as well. I do know, Elaine, you get a gold star for having read all seven of my published books.

Getting back to questions and answers, I always get asked the question as to why I would give a title in Spanish to a book written in English. The answer is not romantic nor ingenious. When I finished writing the book and setting it up for publication, I became aware of a tee-shirt company online and one of their designs was an ape wearing a beret and looking like a revolutionary.

At that time, the working title for the book was up with Apes. I liked the tee-shirt with the ape revolutionary on it and the caption *Viva La Evolución*. Up with Apes just didn't fit because there was a lot more to this book than just an ape story.

The guy who owned the tee-shirt company and I got into contact with one another and he said he thought that if I named the book *Viva*

La Evolución, people might buy and wear the tee-shirt and that would be free publicity. So, I decided to do it and call it *Viva La Evolución*. He was right. The ape tee-shirt was for sale everywhere and the book tie-in was very good. Hence that is the skinny on how this book got its title.

Your fellow member Emily asked me a very interesting question. She wanted to know what the scariest moment in my life was. I have been asked many questions, but this was a new one. I really hadn't thought about it, so I told her my story about waiting for a bus in Okinawa one night where I came face-to-face with a cobra. I wrote about this incident in my book *Contessa*.

After I got home and started thinking about the different adventures I had in life, I mulled over Emily's question and came up with a different answer. I had been scared by that cobra but that was not the most afraid I had ever been. Let me explain and you can send a copy of this letter to Emily.

In 1961 I went to Madrid to finish working on my master's degree at the University of Madrid. This was my first time in Europe, and I decided that before going to Madrid to study, I should take a few small tours of Europe. I started out with a traveling companion. We did not hit it off all that well, so we split in Munich. He went to Rome and I went to Berlin. In 1961 Berlin was divided into two parts, West Berlin and East Berlin. At the time I arrived in Berlin there was no Berlin Wall that separated the two from one another. People, tourists mainly, could travel between the two cities. I was staying in a rather nice hotel in West Berlin which had recuperated quite nicely since the war. Things were rather expensive and so I had to watch my marks, the German currency. The official rate of exchange then was four Western marks to one US dollar.

I decided to visit East Berlin. It was a bit scary because it was so drab and poor and had not really gotten on the path of rebuilding. I took the subway from West Berlin to East Berlin. There were no formalities. I got off the subway at the heart of East Berlin at a large public square called

Alexander Platz. It was cold and unexciting due to being dimly lit with very few businesses open. I walked around and was approached by a man who asked me if I wanted some Eastern marks. I asked him if the exchange rate was the same. He said no and informed me he was giving ten Eastern marks to the dollar. He was rather nervous, and I had a feeling that I should not be trading money with this man but the thought of ten marks for a dollar got to me, and I gave him ten dollars for a hundred Eastern marks. He disappeared in the dark like some wild spirit.

So, I had a hundred Eastern marks, but I did not see anything to spend them on. I did finally see a large restaurant which looked nicer than the others in the area. I looked at their posted menu and the prices seemed to be giveaways for their food. I decided to go in and have dinner. The place was sparsely inhabited with customers. I could not read the German menu, so I depended on the waiter for suggestions. He brought out large portions of rather wholesome food. I noticed that most people in the restaurant were eating very little as though the place were super expensive. The table next to mine was inhabited by an elderly couple who were eating just soup. I had all those marks and I could easily afford to buy them dinner. So, I called my waiter and ordered them some dinner. They were very surprised when the wholesome dishes arrived at their table. The waiter explained that I was their benefactor. They thanked me and smiled.

The time came to pay the check. The waiter brought the bill and it amounted to sixty-seven Eastern marks. I gave the waiter four twenties.

The elderly couple left and nodded their thanks to me. As I was about to get up to leave, two plain clothes policemen identified themselves to me in good English. They asked to see my official currency exchange document. One of the policemen gave me a dreadful look when told him I had no such document. He then asked me how many Eastern marks I had. I had twenty which he immediately confiscated. He then asked me in English if I did not know that it was a crime in East Berlin to trade money on the black market. He then put me under arrest.

With my heart in my throat, I was led out of the restaurant with everyone watching. I was taken to police headquarters in East Berlin. I tried to ask the policeman questions, but he said for me to be quiet. We arrived at the police headquarters and I was taken into the booking room. From there I was taken to an interrogation room which was empty except for one chair. They left me alone in the room. A little sliding window would open every so often and then shut vigorously. When I tried to sit in the one chair someone would open the window and say in a loud voice for me to not sit. I was terrified. What had I gotten myself in to? Would I be sent to prison in East Germany?

Conditions remained the same for quite some time and I was extremely tired of standing. All of a sudden, the little sliding window opened and a voice said that I could sit. In about fifteen minutes a man entered the room. He was wearing a nice sport coat and was rather handsome but had a serious look on his face. He was holding my passport. He walked over and asked me in English if I were not aware that it was a crime to secure money on the black market. I was so afraid I could barely speak. I told him that I didn't understand the currency black market.

Then he shook my hand and asked me if I knew where Hattiesburg, Mississippi was. So, I told him it was in southern Mississippi. I then added that my mother had gone to Mississippi Normal College in Hattiesburg. He nodded his head and smiled. He told me he knew that school and that indeed he knew Hattiesburg.

I smiled and asked him if he was an American. With a shake of the head, he indicated he was not. Then he told me that he was a German prisoner of war during World War II and had been in a prison camp located near Hattiesburg. He said the people were very nice to the prisoners. They organized sports activities in the camp and played with teams from several nearby colleges. He was always very impressed with the niceness of the people in that area. He decided that one day if he could help somebody out that had something to do with Hattiesburg, he would. Then, with a big smile, he shook my hand and told me that he was dismissing all charges against me and would put me in a taxi and personally take me back to my hotel in West Berlin. I had never been so scared nor relieved. I thanked him profusely and he told me to never break the law again.

I still shake all over about how close I had come to something terrible happening to me. The most unusual thing about this story is that when I woke up the next morning the East Germans were putting up the Berlin wall which would totally end access between the two cities for many years to come. I left that very day for Madrid and certainly vowed never to get myself in such a situation ever again.

So, in my way of thinking, the cobra in Okinawa was terrible but the thought of an East German prison for several years could have been worse.

Pass this along to Emily for me. Thanks, Elaine, for being such a good fan of my books.

Cheers, Jack

Cover of *Viva La Evolución*.

German soccer team in Hattiesburg, MS.

LETTER 27

JERRY

Dear Jerry,

Thank you so much for chasing me down on Facebook. You have been good about keeping in contact over the years. I must admit that I didn't write back as much as I should but, even so, I still have appreciated your thoughts and good wishes over the years. I believe you said in your last letter to me a year or so ago that you were now a grandfather. That is hard to believe being that I taught you in graduate school in the mid-nineties. That sounds like twenty-five years ago. It is a blessing to hold onto friends for such a length of time.

I remember after my first book *Contessa* came out, Lorraine threw a book signing party. It was a very good time. I got asked tons of questions, you being at the front of the line. You were never shy about asking questions and I guess I was never shy about answering them. I do remember your asking me who my three favorite teachers were. You said you asked that because there had to be influences on a student to give them encouragement to attempt writing a book.

If I remember correctly I told you that I had three teachers who taught me a lot about teaching and just living in general. The first was Maria Caso who was one of my teachers at the University of Mexico. She was in her early seventies but still quite active. She made teaching fun and an art in its execution. When she talked, you could see that she enjoyed life and all its joys and mysteries. I remember her telling me in her Spanish grammar class that education was the art of perpetual discovery. I always remembered that because she put such zest into that which she was teaching. Spanish grammar is not the easiest nor most fascinating of subjects but she made it sound like a trip to visit *Alice in Wonderland*. I vowed if I ever taught I would try to be a Maria Caso. Her brother was a famous archaeologist and had discovered the Oaxaca's Monte Alban ruins in southern Mexico. So, each class was like an adventure in living.

The second teacher, believe it or not, was also a Spanish grammar teacher but this one was at the University of Madrid. Her name was Elena Catena and she was a whirlwind. She was not feminine and more like an athletic coach. Her first words to our class were, "You wouldn't think this one could be a mother, would you?" She laughed with more energy than I ever remember seeing in a classroom. She went through the rules of Spanish grammar as though they were a football game. She remarked once that teaching and learning were both pure energy. Without energy, you are lost in the teaching profession. She inspired me to be active in life, not passive, and be fun and interesting at the same time. She was a wonder, I can tell you that.

The last of my three was my speech teacher at Mississippi State University. This particular teacher's name was Charles Lawrence but everyone called him Pappy, for what reason I still don't know. He was a very large, distinguished man. I kind of dreaded taking his class because I thought it was going to be one of those places where your grade counted on how much you brown-nosed the professor. To my complete surprise, Pappy did not have an imposing ego of any kind. He was like a combination of Maria Caso and Elena Catena. He made the art of learning fun and he truly enjoyed life. The speech course could be a kind of personality contest, but he never approached it like that as a teacher or with his students. He had energy and made every day fun enough to celebrate in one way or another. I certainly learned a terrific amount on being out in public that was completely attributable to this gentleman.

So that brings us, Jerry, to you and me. As one of my students I remember you were a handful as a lot of people said. You were rather aggressive in manner and asked far too many questions. However, I was well seasoned enough to handle you and/or questions thanks to Maria, Elena and Pappy. So we got along just great. See, something must have stuck or you wouldn't be writing me after twenty-five years. You were a very active person and that is what I had to offer you as your teacher.

I taught high school Spanish for a few years in California. Most language courses at the time were places you studied for a test and would never speak the language. Life was just one grammar rule and exercise after another. When I first started my classes, I looked at the textbook and saw nothing that would excite anybody. It was all a drill in futility. I decided that my students were going to speak Spanish, not treat it as a dead language. I wrote some plays and divided the class into groups, and we performed those plays and then had awards for best actor, best actress, etc. It was tough and students had to know the Spanish but they did get into it and at least they were speaking Spanish in the end, not dealing in boredom.

I remember waiting in line at a Mexican restaurant in Los Angeles. All of a sudden in my ear was whispered "Es un licantropo." This is a line for one of my plays about werewolves. The sentence translates to, "It's a werewolf." I turned around and standing there was a very nice looking gentleman with a lady and a young man. I had to think a moment when he then said, "Hi Señor's Fitzgerald. It is Ronnie, the most noisy kid in your classes." Then I recognized him. Yes, it was Ronnie, a former language student and after all those years he did remember a line from that Spanish werewolf play. He said he was a doctor and then introduced me to his college age son and wife. He told them that I was his favorite teacher from many years ago. That was really a rewarding night.

So, here you have it, Jerry. This is who I became in the teaching business as well as the writing business. Very best and I promise to answer your letters more promptly.

Sr. Jack Fitzgerald

LETTER 28

JUNE LEE

Dear June Lee,

It was so good to hear from you and your catching me up on everyone in your family. I do remember when your mother was alive and what a kick she was. She had a great personality and was a great friend. I can hardly believe that you have a son in college. The last time I looked I think he was something like two years old. It certainly shows how fast time flies.

I was happy to have you remember my birthday. I simply cannot believe I am eighty-nine years old but, again, that just show you how fast time goes by.

In your letter you mentioned that your son, Rick, was majoring in creative writing and is already in his third year at college. You wanted some information on what it is like to actually try to make a living as a writer so you could help prepare Rick for the days when he will try to enter the profession. I laugh a little bit here because your mom once asked me the same thing and she said that she wanted to hear how I got by in life as a writer without the usual "varnish and toro poo-poo," as she called it.

So, I will try to mention a few things I have learned since jumping into the creative world and trying to make a go of it. First of all, some people are very lucky, some are so-so lucky, and others are not lucky at all.

I fit in the medium group which means where most professional writers are. I am not one of the masters of writing like Stephen King et al. They are the lucky ones. People in my category have ups and downs, valleys and peaks or just plain good times and bad times. If you fall into the hard luck of would-be authors, it would be prudent to look for an allied profession where you won't starve to death. Valleys and peaks mean that times can be rough and you have to go with the flow and work your way to some better time. One big thing though is you must have the hide of a rhinoceros from the get-go and can take rejection and somehow keep going. I can well remember one such period in my life. I was the writer on a screenplay project at Paramount Studios. Life was a bowl of cherries. Then one day out of the blue things fell apart due to creative differences with the producer and some actors and the next thing I knew I was out on the street looking like a cat crying for cheese, as my Aunt Nanny Lou used to say. She meant that one was poor.

I was living in Los Angeles and it was not easy to pay rent, eat, or make car payments, etc. with nothing coming in and not having put enough away for a rainy day. I quickly had to do something to try and bring in something as part time jobs were rare as hummingbird teeth. The first idea I had was to put an ad in the LA Times advertising myself as a tutor of French, Spanish, and English as a foreign language. From that ad I got exactly four students. That would bring in something but just barely enough to keep me going. Also during such times, friends are far and few because they don't want to take you on as a liability. You do what it takes to survive and try again or give up and get into another profession. In my case as I say, I had four students. This wasn't all that good because part time independent work like this is just keeping you at a valley. Besides, you can never tell how reliable such students are. So, you give it your best until you find something or give up. Rick must realize that this is the way it is for most people when they start out writing.

My first student was a German lady who came to California with her husband who was a doctor. He was taking a specialty course at the UCLA Medical Center. She spent her days shopping and sightseeing. So, we played shopping. I would be the clerk and she the customer. Her English was limited so it was fun for me to pretend and learn at the same time. She lasted two weeks.

Student number two was a young lady who wanted to swap her expertise for my expertise. She considered herself a clairvoyant and gave readings. She also ran prosperity sessions where her proteges made-up prosperity posters. They would cut things out of magazines and post them on a poster board and meditate with her for their realization. Sometimes they did guided imagery. She would talk and they would imagine prosperity in all adventures of their life. Anyway, I told her that she probably was quite successful and could easily pay for her French lessons. She wanted to study French because she wanted to go to Paris where she heard people would sign up for her prosperity lessons. She did finally come through with some money for me and the two of us did some minor French. She wanted only some key sentences explaining her wares. She and I role-played these sessions. She would give her spiel and I would be the French pigeon who asked her simple questions in French. She lasted three weeks.

Then student three was a flight attendant who wanted to brush up on her Spanish so she could apply for a South American position as a flying waitress or should I say attendant. We role-played hostess and flyer in Spanish. She quickly became quite good. And too quickly because she only lasted two weeks.

Student four was a young man who wanted to learn show business French. He said he was working on a film and would soon be working on a film about Basque immigrants to the state of Nevada. These people mainly spoke French and needed to know key words for his assistant producer role. He actually lasted about six weeks. One day we were doing role playing of simple questions in French as though he were conducting an interview. I looked at him while he was answering and I told him he looked familiar to me and if we had ever met previously. He said no and we continued. In asking questions to him down the line, I found out he was the son of two famous actors, Joel McCrea and Francis Dee. Then I told him the reason I thought he looked familiar. Anyway, he was a very good student and a quick learner. During our time together I mentioned that I was a writer who was at liberty as the saying goes. He was curious and asked if I had any scripts that I had written which he could read. I gave him two of mine. A week or so later he reported to me that not only had he read the scripts but he had let his father read them. It turned out that his father and mother were to be in a motion picture based a book by the Laxalt family in Nevada. He was the governor of Nevada and his brother was a writer and had written the book the movie was based on. He said that they were having trouble with the writer of the screenplay who had promised to have the screenplay ready in six weeks but it was now three months and he hadn't even started. So, they fired him. They offered me the job of writer on the project. I accepted and was quickly out of the dumpster and back on Main Street.

So that is how it goes, June Lee. Unless you are a brand name in this business, you can expect to live a life with many ups and downs. That is about the max I can give your son, Rick, as far as the nuts and bolts of the writing game. My best of luck to him and I think maybe you have some insight to pass on to him when he tries his hand at this profession.

Very best to you,
Cheers, Jack

LETTER 29

BUZZ

Hi Buzz,

Sorry I had to cancel our lunch engagement the other day but Mother Nature decreed that I stay at home and deal with some bad side effects from a little white Devil pill which the doctor gave me to help control my glaucoma. In fact, that little white pill was no fun. It took me nearly a week to get over with the doctor telling me to stop taking the little monsters. I am almost back to normal and hope that we can get together as soon as the all-clear claxon sounds in my system. I had intended to continue my story in person about the second time I lived in Mexico. So, hopefully, this email will fill in and when we do next see one another, I can answer all your questions.

The second time I lived in Mexico was after I got out of the Army. I had intended to continue at Mississippi State College but heard about a new school that had opened up in Mexico City called Mexico City College. It was accredited by the Education Department of the State of Texas. I checked with the registrar at Mississippi State to see if such credits were transferable toward my degree. They investigated and told me all would be okay.

I figured that it would be pretty good to go to Mexico City and spend a year on the G.I. Bill and at least come back to the university with a minor in Spanish.

Believe it or not, I had been told about Mexico City College by a student at State who was from the Soviet Union. The story was that he found a college catalogue some place in Moscow and managed to get on a student exchange program. He ended up at Mississippi State and I found him quite the character. Boris was lively, a big walrus of a guy, and was good and friendly to one and all. Everybody loved him. He worked in the college bookstore and made it a fun place to go.

Before Boris went to work there the bookstore was just about as interesting as a pie eating contest. The couple who ran the bookstore were okay but Boris was the main attraction. He was just on all the time. The couple apparently felt sorry for him and gave him a place to stay and a little income.

Boris and I had coffee several times since we belonged to the International Club at State that was composed of foreign students and those who were interested in foreign affairs. When Boris heard of my interest in Spanish he told me about this school opening in Mexico City and said I should check into it. So, Boris was the one who put the thought in my head. Before I knew it, I had been accepted at Mexico City College and I thanked Boris for all his help.

I went to Mexico City and began attending classes that summer. The year was 1956. There was no dorm at Mexico City College. They did have a housing office that would hook you up with a nice home where one could live. I met a very pleasant Mexican woman who said that she had a place for two students in her home. In the housing office at the same time I was there was a young man from Chicago named Sam. We decided to rent her two rooms as the price was right and included two meals every day and laundry. What could go wrong?

Sam and I moved in. We enjoyed our classes at MCC yet from the get go we realized we were not in a regular situation in the lady's home. It turned out that the pleasant Mexican woman was married to a Russian named Vladimir whom she called Vladi. He had been part of the Russian Revolution and had come to Mexico to escape the Red Army. He was in the White Army of the Russian revolution. He had stories galore of his part in the revolution and how he had to escape with his life following the leader of the White Russian Army.

That leader had been murdered in Mexico. The story was that a newspaper man came to interview him. During the interview he took out a hatchet and murdered the White Army leader. Vladi then went into hiding for many years, married, and had a family. He was a very interesting person but always had to look over his shoulder in case someone was lurking to give him the same hatchet treatment.

Sam and I did not really feel safe in the home. The Señora did all she could to make us feel welcomed and so did Vladi, but we just didn't like being in the middle of such unusual goings on. We found another very nice apartment in the Polanco area of Mexico City. It was in the European section the city and had all sorts of nice shops and activities. What we found was a private home with two apartments upstairs built over the garage. The price was right and the woman who owned the place worked at some government office. She got us a full-time maid for twenty-eight dollars a month who did some cooking, the laundry, and cleaning. We were having a great time.

In the apartment next to ours lived a woman named Ruth and her husband Bart. They had a long-haired Pomeranian dog which was very sweet and friendly. Ruth and Bart occasionally would meet us out on the patio where we would have drinks, chat, and pet the dog named Mr. Pete. Ruth was an American but Bart was of some unknown foreign extraction whose English and Spanish were serviceable but not what you would call fluent. Even so, Sam and I were enjoying the good life. One night we were out on the patio having drinks and it was about time to go to bed. We heard a lot of rustling in the nearby big trees. I wondered what was going on over there. Ruth laughed and said that was where the poor people lived. They could not afford homes, so they slept in the trees. Sounds incredible but nevertheless those shaken limbs and leaves were heard every night.

All was going great until one fateful night there was a lot of noise and shuffling from Ruth and Bart's apartment. It definitely was not coming from the trees. Very quickly all became silent. I didn't think anything more of it and went back to sleep. The next morning there was a loud banging on the front door. I answered the door and several men and policemen were there. They asked if I or Sam had seen the neighbors that morning. I said I had not but that there had been lots of noise over in that apartment the preceding night. Sam and I were told that we had to go to police headquarters and be interrogated. We could not imagine what was going on but went with them. As things developed, we were told that Ruth and Bart ran a large Soviet spy ring that operated from Mexico City. They had been found out and had escaped and supposedly had gone to Cuba. I was totally shocked. First Vladi and all his history and now Ruth and her stories. The people at the police station said the only thing left in Ruth's apartment was their Pomeranian, Mr. Pete. They asked if we could take care of the dog and we said we would.

At the time the newspapers were filled with stories of this spy ring. Believe it or not, the entire spy ring included London, Mississippi State, Mexico City, and Cuba. Yes, I said Mississippi State. But it turns out that Boris from the bookstore was head of the spy ring that was checking on the large US Air Force Strategic Air Command base that was located in Columbus, Mississippi, just ten miles from Mississippi State. The bookstore manager and his wife were also part of Boris' operation as well as an elementary school teacher living in Columbus. The scandal caused the fall of one government in London due to spies operating out of there.

As you can see, Buzz, my second trip to Mexico was extremely unusual. I am sure you are going to have a ton of questions to ask me about all of this. So, there you have some details about my second stay in Mexico. I have one more. It too is highly unusual, but I will have to save it for another lunch meeting.

Cheers and best to you,
As always, Jack

LETTER 30

SARAH GEORGE

Dear Sarah George,

Thanks for your birthday card and phone call. I can always count on you to wish me well. We go back far when we first met at Woodbury University. I was a part time communications teacher in the graduate program, and you were a counselor. I do remember all the fun conversations we had, especially during coffee breaks. I remember when we first met you told me your dad was somewhat eccentric because he wanted a boy so bad that he named you George with your grandmother's name tacked on to honor her. I have always appreciated your sense of humor and you do find funny cards to send on my birthday. I think one of the things I remember most about you is that you told me once that if you had some situation in which you could save only one set of entities in your life, you would choose your three dogs rather than your three children. You said the dogs were always happy to see you. They never argued with you and their affection was all encompassing. That got me to thinking over the pets in my life.

I think I told you about a cocker spaniel that was a real part of my life for a dozen years. When I was fifteen I got it in my mind that I wanted a cocker spaniel. My Aunt Helen in Detroit had a black cocker named Lady and I thought it was the best dog ever.

In Okolona, dogs were plentiful, but they were all just dogs. As puppies they were cute but grew up to be just mutts. Even so, they were loving, and they looked at us only with love and affection. No one had anything but just dogs, what my mother called them. I remember when I was younger, someone would pawn a puppy off on me. I would take it home and my mother would tell me to take that dog right back where you got it. In those days no one spayed a dog and so puppies were much too plentiful. Rare was the dog that had a pedigree or some standing.

I remember though that someone gave my father a grown Water Spaniel which they had to get rid of because its owner had died. My father brought it home and we all fell in love with this dog which we named Spunky. I had never seen such a smart dog. Most ordinary dogs were not prone to learn tricks or commands or even much English. However, Spunky took to us as much as we took to him.

As I write this, I am remembering things that happened with Spunky that were incredible and at this point in my life I have a hard time believing.

After we had Spunky for about three years, the bonding between us and Spunky was as solid as could be. Even so, an engineer at the railroad where my father worked saw Spunky and offered my father a hundred dollars for the dog. In those days a hundred dollars was a fortune and especially in our household.

Much to my pleading as well as others in my family, my father took the hundred dollars and gave Spunky over to the care of the engineer. We missed Spunky but soon life goes on and one gets new problems and interests in life.

One day I went out to the back of our house and, much to my total surprise, there was Spunky. He looked almost wasted and in very bad shape. We nursed him back to health as well as we could.

It turned out the engineer lived in Meridian, Mississippi, about a hundred and fifty miles from Okolona. The engineer informed my father that Spunky had run away about three months ago and he thought he probably had gotten killed. Now he was in Okolona and was as delighted to see us and we were to see him. My father offered to return the hundred dollars to the engineer, but he said that any dog that would travel that distance and managed to come back home to us was special and that he would not take the money back.

I think I was the most upset about Spunky. Here was a dog that looked at you and you felt total communication of love. It was hard to explain. I was just heartbroken when Spunky died.

I began badgering my parents for another Spunky. I looked in the ads in the *Commercial Appeal* from Memphis under "Pets for Sale." My parents said that money was too tight to be able to spend for a dog when puppies were plentiful just for the asking. No, I wanted a Cocker Spaniel or Water Spaniel. I saw an ad selling a Cocker Spaniel puppy for twenty-five dollars. I really pushed to try and see if I couldn't persuade my folks to get me that dog. My brother Paul was in the Navy at the time, and he ended up advancing the twenty-five dollars for the dog. It was so exciting waiting for those people from Memphis, a hundred miles from Okolona, to bring me the puppy.

One fine weekend the Memphis people showed up with what I thought was the cutest puppy I had ever seen. It was red and instantly the two of us fell in love. It was a female, so I chose the name Scarlett for her. I made a leash, and we would walk daily together. At that time in Okolona, regular dogs didn't come into the house. They stayed outside and that is where you fed them and connected with them. It was pretty unheard of to have a dog stay inside one's home. Spunky had visitation rights to come in for a while but Scarlet was never left outside alone.

To this day I cannot understand how a dog and a human can bond so effectively as I had with Spunky and now Scarlett. What a great time we had together. People thought the Fitzgeralds had lost their mind paying twenty-five dollars for a dog.

Scarlett was as smart as a whip and I was certain that we understood one another when I talked. She was so very sweet. People thought I was some foolish little sissy walking my dog on a leash. Anyway, someone in the vicinity of Tupelo, which was nineteen miles away, had a red Cocker Spaniel and so we bred them, and Scarlet produced four puppies. Three were red and one was black. My parents were quite delighted because they were able to advertise and sell the three red puppies but the black puppy I wanted to keep. I named him Duke of Okolona but just called him Duke. He was so frisky and full of life that my mother said she could not have two dogs in the house because people would talk. So unfortunately, we had to sell Duke. I was only willing if Scarlett and I had visitation rights, which we did.

Scarlett was so smart. I trained her to go fetch the newspaper every morning, which was delivered at the edge of our property. The paper was folded up. Scarlett would get it and bring it to me and wag not only her tail but her entire body.

I always got home from school about three-thirty in the afternoon. My mother would let Scarlett out and she would go and wait on the corner until she saw me arriving on my bicycle. She was so delighted to see me. Later on, I graduated from high school and went to Mississippi State and other places, but Scarlett went every afternoon waiting for me to arrive. When she felt I was not coming, she reluctantly went back into the house.

I was in the Army for two years and nine months. Two years of that I was overseas stationed on Okinawa. My mother wrote me that every day Scarlett went to the corner and waited for me to come but then would leave when she was sadly disappointed by my non-appearance.

After I was discharged from the Army I returned to Okolona. The bus station was not far from my parents home, so I walked. As I neared our home, I could see Scarlett was waiting for me at the corner. When she saw me, she ran circles and rolled over waiting for me to get close enough to pet her. She jumped into my lap and kissed me, and it was like her dream had come true.

So, Sarah George, I can safely say that I have had some wonderful experiences with the psyche of dogs and their loyalty. It is unbelievable. So, I can see why you made the statement you did about choosing your dogs over your kids. Of course, I know you were kidding but it does go to show you how attached we get to these four-footed creatures.

Thanks again for the card and phone call.

As always,
Jack

LETTER 31

FRANK

Dear Frank,

Thank you for your review of my latest book *Confessions Of A Script Doctor.* I was certainly pleased that you liked it and found it interesting. I also appreciate your sending me birthday wishes. One thing you mentioned in your email concerned my having been in the Army. You said you thought I might have been drafted but the fact is I volunteered. The reason for your confusion was that if one were drafted in those days, you were in for two years. And you had no choice of what you would be doing in the Army. Most draftees were in the infantry which meant that they probably would go overseas to Korea and get shot at. If one volunteered, it was for three years but one had a semi-chance of getting a job where you didn't dodge bullets.

You said you would have thought I was drafted. The answer to that is no, I volunteered. I admit I was thinking something about getting a more prestigious job instead of infantryman but that was not the real reason.

In order to bring you up to speed I would have to start by telling you the real reason I volunteered. It all began in Mexico City. I had gone there to study Spanish grammar at a special school for foreigners run by the University of Mexico. Very few students attended. In my Spanish class, which was from eight to eleven every morning, five days a week, there were only eight students. It was an eclectic group. A woman and her son, an American lawyer, a guy who claimed to be a writer, a guy who was studying archaeology, and two young ladies from Martinsville, West Virginia. The class was fun and was taught by an American lady in her seventies who married a Mexican many years ago. I became good friends with the young ladies, and we had a very good time. One of them, Nancy, was taking voice lessons and practiced only one song, *The Italian Street Song.*

There were eight of us, including me. Nancy and I got to be very good friends. When our three-month class ended, it was time for all to go our separate ways. I could go back to Okolona but I did not want to do that. I thought that at the age of nineteen I'd go to Los Angeles and see if I could break into show business. This was foolish on my part because I had no money or very, very little, and knew no one in California who could help me. I had no relatives there. I was strictly on my own. I discussed this with Nancy and she said that she would loan me money for a bus ticket from Mexico City to Laredo and then bus fare from there to Los Angeles. I assured her I would pay her back when I could.

Our little group all had a goodbye party and it was lots of fun. I left the following day on a Mexican bus to go from Mexico City to the Mexican border town of Ciudad Juarez. I had with me my suitcase and my portable typewriter. I decided that perhaps it would be a good idea if I hitchhiked from El Paso, the other side of Ciudad Juarez, to Los Angles. So, I bought a Greyhound ticket to Las Cruces, New Mexico which is not too far from El Paso. I thought that hitchhiking would be better from there.

So, with my suitcase and portable typewriter, I got out on the highway in Las Cruces and waved my thumb in the air. I had only waited about thirty minutes when a car with three people in it stopped. Three young men who were laughing and carrying on asked me where I was going. I replied that I was on my way to Los Angeles. They said that sounded good to them, so they offered me a ride.

We drove till almost dark, and they turned into a motel. I told them I didn't have money for a motel and that I would sleep in the car if it was okay with them. No, they insisted that I stay with them. That night they went out cruising the town and I stayed in the room and slept. They came back late after having visited some bawdy houses and bars in the small town of El Centro. The next morning we got up and had coffee and doughnuts at a nearby restaurant. Then we were on our way to Los Angeles.

We drove that day and got as far as Gila Bend, AZ. We were pulled over by a policeman. The guys seemed very nervous. The policeman said that we would have to follow him to the police station. It turned out that the three young guys were AWOL from the Army and had stolen the car we were in. The Justice of the Peace sent them off to the poky and looked at me and asked me how I fit into the puzzle. I told him about my time in Mexico and I was hitchhiking to Los Angeles. He asked me how much cash I had and I told him twenty-five dollars which a friend had loaned me. He levied a fine of twenty dollars on me for hitchhiking and being a public nuisance. That left me with five dollars.

I stayed in the courthouse that night with my suitcase and portable typewriter. The next morning a policeman took me to the Greyhound bus station and with my five dollars I bought a ticket as far as it would take me to Los Angeles. It turned out that five dollars would take me to Riverside, CA, which is still a hundred miles from LA. I had no choice since the policeman was waiting for me to buy the ticket and then get on the bus.

I rode to Riverside and had no money for a place to stay or anything to eat. I saw a pawn shop and pawned my typewriter for five dollars and my high school class ring for eighty-five cents. Without the ring and portable typewriter and just my suitcase I was able to buy a ticket from Riverside to Los Angeles. It was a local bus that made dozens of stops but it cost a little over one dollar to get to LA.

Once I hit LA it was getting dark. I was in downtown Los Angeles in a really tough area. I had to have someplace to spend the night. I saw a hotel that looked like it might be cheap and they had a room for two dollars and a quarter. I had a cup of coffee and two doughnuts for dinner. That night in the hotel was probably the worst night I had ever spent. Observing the people living in the hotel, bed bugs biting me, and terrible smells. I couldn't wait until morning.

The next day I left the hotel as quickly as I could. I soon discovered the Pacific and Electric streetcars which were available to go just about anywhere. I spent twenty-five cents and took off for Hollywood. In one way I couldn't believe I was in this fabled place but there I was with not even one dollars left to exist on.

I got off the streetcar in downtown Hollywood. I walked with my suitcase to no place in particular. I had no idea what I was up to in life at this point. I saw an employment agency, went in, and a somewhat friendly guy saw me and my suitcase. He remarked to the other employees that here was yet another orphan coming to Hollywood to find fame and fortune. I told him that all I wanted was a job. He asked me if I could wash dishes and I told him I could and would.

He sent me to Junior's Drive-In twelve miles away in Burbank. The manager of Junior's was not nice, treated me as though I were dirt, told me if I could move my tail fast with washing dishes, I could get seventy-five cents an hour but had to pay full price for anything I ate. I was starving and he treated me to a burger which would cover my first session with the sinks. It was awful. The people in the kitchen were crude and unfriendly. The manager said he had an arrangement with a boarding house across the street where I could stay. So, I jumped into the glamorous world of Junior's. The water was so bad it cracked my hands. My seventy-five cents an hour was eaten up by cheeseburgers and my place to stay in that terrible boarding house. Life was terrible and I lasted only a week at Junior's.

I had about five similar jobs and was slowly getting way behind in just the act of living. I needed to go back to Okolona if I could arrange money via my parents to pay for the bus trip. Then there was the Korean war going on and I was up for the draft. My mother said that I would be drafted at any time.

I was walking past a recruiting office in Hollywood one day and decided to go in. Actually, the recruiting sergeant treated me very nice. I was not used to that. He explained that there were benefits once I got out like the GI Bill and that if I volunteered, I could go into something interesting rather than being a plain infantryman. I definitely did not want to be an infantryman because that sounded like my present life in Los Angeles at the time. When the recruiter told me I would have three meals a day, a good place to sleep, and make seventy-five dollars a month I volunteered immediately. I would beat the draft and this act would definitely keep me out of a terrible lifestyle in which I had fallen. So, Frank, that is why I volunteered to go into the Army. Many people hated military service when they went in, but for me it was like a holiday after all those terrible work experiences in Los Angeles. And as far as trying to break into Hollywood, that would have to wait for some other future time. I just had to get my life into some sort of order and that I did.

My life did change and with the help of the GI Bill benefits I not only got a good education but my life changed into having a decent break in my life. There were certainly things I didn't like about the Army but all I had to do was think of Junior's Drive-In and the Army didn't seem so bad.

Thanks for writing to me.

Best to you,
Cheers, Jack

LETTER 32

BECKY

Dear Becky,

I am so glad that we have gotten into contact with one another. I have not seen you since you were a teenager and you visited us in Okolona. Via Facebook, several relationships have been re-established, mainly people I went to school with or worked with. But you are my first cousin and retired. What is very interesting is that your dad was my father's brother and his wife was Jenny, who recently died at a 103. What is so interesting about our reconnecting after all these years is that my brother Paul has a daughter named Becky, whose mother was Jenny and both Beckys are doctors. Very interesting.

In your most recent letter to me you asked who, in my opinion, was the most interesting person in our family. I am just now getting around to making up my mind on how to answer that question.

Our family is a large one. Our grandparents on our fathers' side were James Willard Fitzgerald and his wife Minnie, our grandmother. Little is actually known about James Willard and Minnie because they died at a rather young age. Little was known about Minnie except that she had eleven children with my father being the youngest. One day our grandfather was driving Minnie and my infant father in his carriage back to their home in Mississippi. A snake appeared in their path. The horse startled and reared up, upsetting the carriage and throwing Minnie out onto the road. My father was also tossed with her but apparently was unharmed. Minnie though was gravely injured and died soon thereafter.

James Willard was a schoolteacher. He had graduated from Syracuse University in New York but due to having so many to feed and care for he found himself in poor health and died when my father was two years old.

Van, the oldest of Minnie and James Willard's children, tried to care for them but had to instead break the family up and place them with other members of the family. The two youngest children were my father Everette and his sister Nanny Lou. Your father stayed with Van while Everette and Nanny Lou went to Minnie's sister in Okolona, Mattie Lyons. They unfortunately lived a rather hard existence as Mattie was a widow with little income outside of selling milk, eggs, butter, and garden vegetables.

Everette went to work as soon as he could and thus was deprived of a formal education. He was self-taught in just about everything including Greek, Latin and Spanish. He worked for the GMN & O Railroad for all his adult life.

Nanny Lou decided at a very early age that she was going to go the route of Wallis Simpson, the Duchess of Windsor. This made her the most interesting member of our family. I must qualify the word interesting because she did not do anything outstanding. She lived a very interesting life any way you look at it. While my father had very little formal education, Nanny Lou went through high school and showed some signs of being a writer, specializing in the writing of poetry.

After high school she took business courses in Memphis, Tennessee, where she learned typing, stenography, and looking for a rich husband, her version of the Duke of Windsor.

She later taught in a girl's school in Canton, Mississippi, where she was in charge of Zouave techniques. This consisted of Greek dances mainly with a hoop the size of a hula hoop. The girls would put on recitals of their Zouave dances. She would go every summer to Allison Wells, a water spa outside of Jackson where she taught modern dance and young lady refinements. She had several interested beaus, but none managed to be well-off enough that she would like to spend her married life as their wife.

Nanny Lou was getting older and not having any luck finding Mr. Right. She indeed did look like The Duchess of Windsor but what she failed to realize was that there was room for only one Duchess of Windsor. Aunt Mattie told her that she should find someone nice and settle down.

Nanny Lou had become a Jack-of-all-trades but a master of none. Her finding Mr. Right was difficult. However, she did finally find a man named Whitfield, who had been a Colonel, or so he said, in World War One. It turned out that Dauby, as she called him, or his real names of Nate and Nathan, was quite a bit like her. Both were looking for the golden life but not finding it. They did work for several newspapers as reporters, her poems being published at intervals in newspapers and magazines.

She came into my life when I was about four years old. She taught me to read before I went to school. She told jokes and funny stories about her and Dauby's experiences. She led a very colorful life and she is the one I would say was the most interesting.

She was witty and really opened up my life to wanting experiences here and there. I realized, though, at an early age, that as much fun as I thought my Aunt Nanny Lou was, I did not want to follow her life.

She and Dauby were traveling salespersons. In their case, he sold men's shoes and suits and she sold hospital garb as well as shoes. They managed to eek out a living but one could never say they lived a dull life. Everybody in the family enjoyed knowing Nanny Lou and she was a fun person to know. My friends thought she was a kick and some of her poems eventually became quite well known. But writing poetry is a very difficult way to make a living.

I guess the one thing I learned from my Aunt Nanny Lou that stuck with me over the years is that she taught me not to be afraid of life. Hence, via her, I always veered toward the interesting and the adventurous in life, thus giving me lots to write about in my books, screenplays, and plays.

Dauby, unfortunately, in their later years was crossing a street in Columbus, Mississippi, and was hit by a drunken driver. He died several days later. Nanny Lou was alone in her adventurous world and her Duke was no longer part of her life.

She ended up in Asheville, North Carolina, living in a room at the Wolf House, a boarding home run by the mother of the very well-known author, Tom Wolfe. This was a great atmosphere for her, and she continued selling hospital garb and other door to door sales items until she retired with a small Social Security check. She visited members of her family and we all loved her visits because of all her talents, which were never truly recognized. I kept in contact with her quite often and she visited me from time to time.

She passed away in the late seventies in Asheville at the Wolfe House. I guess, in so many ways, she was like one of the first hippies. She had a zest for life and truly met life face-to-face in so many situations. I do have fond memories of her. I have put one of her poems here to show you her thoughts. She would be so pleased that you and I are now friends and that you now know a lot about this unknown aunt of yours.

Cheers and very best to you,
Love, Jack

Nanny Lou Poem

Oh! Lovely tree
In your tinsel dress
Your glory was
Short lived at best.

You twinkled and sparkled
Before the glass
A joy to all
Who chanced to pass.

In a few short days
You were carted away
And forlornly in
The trash pile lay.

Your cost in dollars
Was very high
Oh! What a shame
To wilt and die.

Like the heyday of youth
Tis fleet and sure
And for old age
There is no cure.

In a very brief time
You are cast aside
To make room for
The rushing tide.

LETTER 33

CRAIG

Dear Craig,

I haven't heard from you recently, so I thought I'd drop you a line to see if you sold your house. The last I heard was that you had put your house on the market because there were a lot of feral cats in the area. You claimed that they caused noise and were fighting and running across the roof. I got to thinking about feral cats. These cats who belong to nobody are not ever able to be tamed. I don't know that you tried but apparently the problem was such that you had to do something and you just decided that selling the house would be the best solution.

I got to thinking about feral cats. Years ago I accepted a job teaching Spanish at New York State University in Plattsburg. Ken had gotten a position as a French and English teacher at the local high school and we were ready to try and see how living in upper state New York would be.

It turned out that when we got to Plattsburg, we found that there was a rental crunch, meaning that due to no dorms at the university all living was done in apartments. By the time of our arrival most apartments were taken and we had to really look and look for some place to live.

We contacted a real estate agency run by a man and his wife. They took pity on us and rented us a farmhouse on the outskirts of Plattsburgh in a community called Morrisonville. They planned to move into the place the following year and said that they would rent the place for one year. The farmhouse was very nice and was two stories which gave us each room to spread out. Mrs. Gerry told us that the barn at the far edge of the property was full of feral carts. At the time I had no real idea what was going on in the world of feral cats. At that time a cat was just a cat.

We got settled in and the autumn was very nice but we could tell winter was on its way. We walked down to the barn every so often to see these feral cats in action. There were kittens of every age, but all looked afraid of us as though we were the devil himself. We took some food down to try and make friends with them but talk about skittish, they vanished every time we went. However, they soon got used to our arriving with some treats.

One time we went about thirty-five miles to Montreal. It was a way to spend several days and then to Quebec to see the changing of the leaves. I have never seen such a beautiful area with all those golden and red and orange leaves.

We left a bag of cat food for the Gerry's to put out for our feral cat population. However, due to a mix-up, they put all the food out at once and stray dogs got to it. When we returned from our trip, we went to check on our feral cat population and even though they were wild by nature they let us know they were super hungry.

We thought that we could lure them to the house so that is where we put out the food. Yes, they did come up to the house. We actually made friends with a couple of the cats and they would come and spend some time with us but their wild nature called them back to the barn.

One of them we called Lapin, which means rabbit in French, because he looked like a rabbit with some black patches on white. He was very nice but was half tamed and half wild. Another totally black cat which we called Winston took our food and would actually let us pet him a bit but he too would run back to his haven in the barn.

Our year passed with a terrible winter and it turned out we had to feed the cats through such a stark time.

We hated to leave at the end of our year in Plattsburg but were off to Mexico and could not carry a cat with us. We did take Lapin back to Mississippi to live with my mother. She had a very sweet cat named Lucy which Lapin almost hissed so hard it blew her hair sideways. So, she couldn't stay with my mother. Ken decided to take her to live with his grandmother. However, on the way to Oklahoma, he let Lapin out of the car to go to the bathroom. All of a sudden, Lapin disappeared. Being in the wild took over and we never saw him again.

Then I got to thinking of a trip to Turkey I took some years ago. We went to Ephesus the place of the ancient Roman ruins. This is one of the most beautiful treasures of ancient buildings. However, what took my notice was the number of cats I saw here. I asked the guide and he said they were all friendly. They were feral but they loved people because they were used to the treats that people would give them.

I did not walk around like the other tourists in the group because of problems with my right leg. So, I would sit and look over the ruins. While sitting, there a calico cat came up and jumped into my lap and purred and rolled over and made me think that we had been friends forever. I simply could not believe it but all the kitties here were sweet and acted as tough they were hired to be nice to the tourists.

My calico was enjoying some parts of a sandwich I was eating and which we finished together. The calico kitty was very sweet but all of a sudden acted as though it heard something. I thought its wildness had kicked in but no, I found out that a Russian group of tourists were arriving and apparently they had lots of tidbits to feed the kitties. Miss Calico gave me a quick rub and was off to work the Russian group.

The area had some wild dogs and they too were super friendly. They were different from the cats in that they were like trained dogs and did their best to entertain you.

They were friendly but they weren't up for petting. They were something else. There was this one hound who would sit with us while the tourist guide was telling all about the ruins. The dog listened for a while as though he were a tourist and then started doing tricks like rolling over, making faces at people, etc. The tour guide finally had to chase him off saying he couldn't put up with the competition.

We left one area to go to another area in a wagon. A Chinese woman was eating a sandwich. Everyone stood and when we arrived at our destination, the dog had followed us. While this Chinese woman was munching away on her sandwich she stepped down from wagon. The dog came up to her and ran his cold nose up under her dress and she dropped the sandwich. The dog picked up her sandwich and with one flip of his head was on his merry way to eat it.

These animals were something else and certainly did not seem feral. They were for sure super independent and ran their lives as though they worked for the tourism department. They certainly added some fun to my visit at Ephesus.

So, Craig, there you have my feral cat take on things. I hope you did sell your house and solved the problem caused by all of those wild cats.

Cheers and look forward to hearing back from you.
Jack

Ephesus theater in Turkey.

LETTER 34

MARK

Dear Mark,

Thanks for the birthday card. Rarely do we get a real card these days. More than likely if we do get a card, it is an electronic card but some of those can be quite beautiful and nice. However, there's still something refreshing about a card you can hold in your hand and touch. Thanks again for remembering my birthday.

You signed your card "to a person who has lived a charmed life." That is a great compliment and in certain adventures I have been lucky and lived a charmed life. Even so, it reminds me of people who tell how much they have won at casinos. What they fail to mention though is how much they have lost to get those winnings. That is exactly how I view my life. To win some, I had to go through a lot of unpleasantness. So, even though I realize you are being very nice to tell me I have lived a charmed life, that is not the full story.

I will give you two examples of how life can operate for someone playing in the casino of life. So here are some of the losses. Before I became a writer on what one could call a full-time basis, meaning actually making a living writing, I was trying to be an actor.

I did extra work in many films, some TV commercials and some small parts in movies that unfortunately have evaporated over the years. I just did not have the luck to make it as an actor. I don't know what it was, I did not get hold of the brass ring, as they say.

A lot of people spend fortunes on acting lessons and workshops, and some make it from those but I didn't. I tried them on a limited basis, but my money practically flew out the window with no gain. The way to get into show business as an actor seemed to boil down to the following: join workshops, get an acting teacher, do extra work, and appear in as many showcases as possible. The latter means to appear in a play where you got no money. It eats up your time. You send out photos and resumés hoping to attract someone to come and see you and offer you your chance.

I appeared in several productions at a theater-in-the-round run by a woman and her husband in Glendale, CA. We rehearsed for about three weeks and appeared Thursday through Sunday for six weeks. All you got were the left-over doughnuts and coffee they didn't sell at intermission.

Even so, you had to work your way up with these people. You started out at the bottom of the totem pole with a very small part and if you were good, they promoted you to a better part. I was with them for over a year doing plays. I went from three speaking lines up to the lead in one of their plays called *I Like It Here*, in which I played Willy, an immigrant who was kind of like a Mr. Belvedere, a jack-of-all-trades. It was a good part and I even affected a kind of German accent for the role. The reviews in the local throwaway papers came in and I got mentioned very highly. I thought I was riding high.

One night after a performance a woman in a very exotic costume-type dress and hat asked to see me. She said that I was very good and that she ran an acting agency and that she would like to represent me. She gave me her very nice calling card and scheduled a day for me to come to her office in the Ralph Edwards building on the tenth floor in Hollywood. My parents were visiting me at the time from Mississippi and they were rather excited that after all my work, I was being given an opportunity to get my foot in the door in the acting business. So, on the appointed date of my interview with the lady I went with my parents for my appointment. They waited at a café on the ground floor while I went up to see what fate had in store for me.

I went up to the tenth floor but could not find the lady's office. I went into another office and asked, and they laughed and said that the woman did not exist here. Her offer was just a scam getting her jollies preying on the hopes and wishes of people like me. I had to go back downstairs and reluctantly face my parents with the bad news. They could not understand such a person. I could not understand how my disappointment would be someone else's enjoyment.

I went back to doing Willy at the Glendale Center Theatre and had to tell everyone that my break was nothing but a sham. Everyone there was as disappointed as I was. Apparently, this woman pulled the same act all over the Hollywood area. I never saw her again but thought of what I might say if our paths ever crossed again. As I said, so on with Willy.

Two weeks later another woman wanted to speak to me after the show. I thought it might be that previous witch but no, this was a somewhat unkempt, stout looking woman who introduced herself as Lottie Horner. She produced a card and said she would like to talk with me about taking this show to Broadway. After my first big disappointment, I was not in the mood for any more tricksters. However, the people who ran the theater said that the woman was legitimate and had produced quite a few things on Broadway.

We made a date to meet at her house a few days later. She had three men who seemed to work for her as assistants and I still could not get any enthusiasm built up over this Lottie Horner person.

On the day of our appointment, I drove into the Hollywood Hills via Laurel Canyon and found her address which was the former home of Errol Flynn. It was very elaborate but had been allowed to run down a bit.

I went into her place wondering what might happen next. I was very leery because it was like letting the same dog bite me twice.

The guys who had been with her at the theater met me at the door and took me in. Lottie, they said, would receive me in a few minutes because she was on the phone. I waited and waited and finally she came out, wearing the same outfit she had worn to the play. She was unkempt and smoked and drank. I smoked at the time, but I didn't drink and so just took a soft drink.

Lottie then began. She took out some papers and gave them to me. I looked at them and then asked her what these were. She said they were a contract. She had contacted the author of the play and was indeed going to produce it on Broadway starring of all people me. I didn't know what to say except thank you. She then went over some items and told me I would start on salary as soon as she had concluded the purchase of the stage play. She told me to get my stuff together for the move to New York. She told me she would contact me in a few days with details and to give me my first check.

I could not believe my good fortune. I telephoned my parents, and they were overjoyed. I told people at the theater and they were so pleased that I had finally gotten a chance as it meant that they too might get a role in a play on Broadway.

I went to my apartment and gave notice. My friends there gave a celebratory party and I just couldn't believe all this was happening to me.

I continued playing Willy and I didn't hear from Lottie in a week or so. I tried calling her, but no one answered. Suddenly, my heart sunk into my loafers. That night one of the cast members came in with a copy of the *Hollywood Reporter*, the daily show-business periodical. It had the obituary of Lottie Horner who had died of a heart attack. I drove to her house, but no one was there. No men, no nothing. In fact, I never heard another word from anyone. So, there I was, at square one, again.

These two stories certainly shook my timbers about going forward into show business. That is when I started thinking of trying writing instead of acting. Writing was just as hard to get my toe in the door. Writing didn't really happen for me until ten years later when I was living in Paris, France.

So, my good friend Mark, thanks again for the birthday card. As you can see, I have not had that easy a time of getting my foot through the door in this game of life.

Take care,
Jack

LETTER 35

BUZZ

Dear Buzz,

Yes, yes, I know I owe you a letter. I meant to get back to you earlier, but I am bushed at the moment trying to answer and thank people for their birthday cards and greetings to me. I know I was telling you about my three experiences of living in Mexico. I think I managed to get two emails to you but forgot about the third one, which I will fill you in on with today's letter.

During my ten years in Paris, I founded the Paris English Theater, which mainly existed to showcase my plays. I know it sounds egotistical, but I could not see where I could get ahead by producing other people's plays while mine stayed in a drawer. I did have good success overall with the Paris English Theater.

Toward the end of my ten years in Pairs, my last play produced there was called *Tijuana Lady*. The play had to have a small film introduction. I had no idea how to do such a thing, so I approached the drama critic for the *International Herald Tribune*, Thomas Quinn Curtis, for help. He had given me good reviews and I felt I knew him well enough to ask for help.

He introduced me to a film maker by the name of Wallace Potts, who was the partner of the ballet dancer Rudolph Nureyev, and they were friends with the Oscar winning cinematographer Nestor Almendros. The little film came off very well and the play was quite successful. A British film company optioned it for a film.

One of the people who helped me make the little film was an Italian-Mexican living in Paris and the last partner of Visconti, the great Italian film director of *Death in Venice*. Giuseppe Hibler, the Italian-Mexican film maker was quite helpful in all phases of the production of the little film and the play.

Giuseppe was approached during the run of the play by a Mexican woman named Irma Salinas concerning hiring me to write a screenplay for her. I told Giuseppe that I knew nothing about writing a screenplay, but he was the type who never says never. He said, "Of course you do," and told the woman I would do it. She flew to Paris from her home in Monterrey, Mexico, to see my play and speak to me about her project.

It turned out that Irma was a writer, having written two books and a lot of newspaper columns. She was one of the heirs of Salinas y Rochaq, a chain of stores much like Sears and Roebuck. She was married to a Señor Salinas who came from one of the richest and most powerful families in Mexico. He died accidentally but she smelled foul play. She wrote two books based on her experiences with her husband and his family and decided she wanted a screenplay made. Her family and his family were not friends and there was almost a war going on between the two rich families. Again, Giuseppe insisted that I work with her if she offered me the job.

Indeed she did offer me the job of turning her two books into a screenplay for Paramount Pictures which was to be produced by two Broadway producers, Fritz Hold and Barry Brown, who had done *La Cage aux Folles*. Everything was going so fast I could hardly keep up with it. The plan was for me to leave Paris and move to Acapulco and live in one of her twelve villas there. She would be in her super home in Aspen, Colorado, with bodyguards etc. It all sounded like a movie itself and at Giuseppe's insistence, I accepted. I asked Giuseppe what he wanted out of the situation. He said he would like for me to also write a screenplay for him. I would give it to him and receive nothing for it, no screen credit or money. It seemed like more than a good deal.

So off I went to Mexico and lived in that villa of hers in Acapulco which was super living as well as going occasionally to Aspen to show her how I was coming along. I got this job mainly because I knew Spanish and could turn it into a screenplay in English.

Barry and Fritz were great people to work with too. However, Martin Jurow, who had done *Terms of Endearment*, was brought aboard. I tried pleasing him but we just didn't hit it off all that well. I just did not have the experience in screenplay writing to suit him, which was the truth. At the same time, I was doing this, the screenplay I was writing on the sly for Giuseppe was finished.

I delivered the script to one and all concerned, and things were going quite well. I gave Giuseppe his freebie screenplay which I called, *The Devil Sent You To El Paso*.

Things were going great and I was living high on the hog as they say. Then, overnight, the entire project collapsed. Irma and her in-laws made peace but the price was to destroy the screenplay and have it not be produced. So, there I was, going from living like a pasha to landing on the curb with nothing much to show for the whole experience but a lot of memories. Giuseppe took my script and said it was far too long and so he sold one section of it and made it into a film called *Over Her Dead Body*, or, *Enid is Sleeping*. I got no credit and no money. The movie came off quite well though. Copies can still be bought on Amazon.

All was not lost though because Giuseppe had inherited from Visconti the rights to a project based on the life of Beethoven. Giuseppe said he would pay me to turn it into a short film. There was a film there but not the over three-hundred-page script Visconti had left him. It turns out that Beethoven was an old lech who lusted after his nephew and it ended up a tragedy in that the young man did himself in. These are all things about

Beethoven that most people, including myself, didn't know. So, I took his offer and turned out a normal sized script called *Beethoven's Nephew*. It was filmed but did not meet with much success. I got no credit but I did get money and was told that it would happen more times than not. It was a way to pay rent. So, I have ghost-written quite a few things in my time and whistled as I deposited the check into my account but never receiving much credit for quite a few projects.

So, Buzz, there is the last Mexican Connection I have. Believe it or not, I have not been to Mexico in many, many years. For sure though, Mexico occupies a warm spot in my heart. So, there you have my wrap-up of my Mexican adventures.

Cheers,
Jack

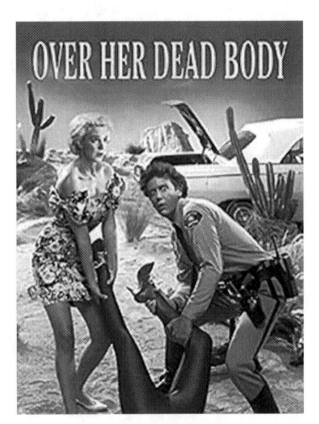

Film *Over Her Dead Body.*

LETTER 36

CHRISTY

Dear Christy,

Thanks for your nice letter. I am sorry that I overlooked your birthday but being that it and Christmas are only one day apart, it appears one's mind during this time frame is more on Santa Claus than birthdays. If one forgets that Christmas itself is the celebration of a birthday. I got your Christmas card also with the photos of all of you. The two girls are growing and are now young ladies, not girls. You mentioned how advanced they were in their acrobatic endeavors. They must have inherited a bit of that from their great-grandfather, my father. He installed a trapeze between two tall cedar trees on our property where I grew up. He would swing on it and did his best to get my brother, your father-in-law, Dorothy, my sister-cousin, and me to give it a try. Dorothy was very good at it and Paul was pretty good at it and I was not interested. I could see a swing but not a trapeze. It looked too dangerous to me.

During this period I was fourteen years old and in the ninth grade at school. Paul was a senior in high school and Dorothy was in college. The item that interested me was that a black minstrel company called *F. W. Woolcott Minstrel Show* was coming to Okolona, my hometown. This was something because we only had a population of two thousand people but more blacks than whites. They had advance public posters pasted all over Okolona and to me, with my dreams of somehow wanting to be in show business, I did not want to miss such an opportunity.

Ellen, our black housekeeper, with whom I spent many hours in conversation, told me all about it. They would have black comedians, dancing girls and all sorts of singing. She said that she had seen this group once before and said they had a big cast, lots of good musicians playing wonderful music and it would be quite a performance. The good part of it, she told me, was that half of the audience seating was for whites and the other half was for blacks.

I mentioned to my family that I wanted to attend but my mother said she didn't think so. This hit me like a ton of bricks. She had no interest in attending and since we did not own a car, we would have to walk to get there, and I just couldn't do that by myself at night. My father worked the swing shift at the railroad, and he couldn't because of working. Dorothy would not be home from college at that time. Paul was going steady with a girl named Donna and they were out at Wilson Park in the pavilion at a high school dance.

Ellen was probably one of the nicest people I have ever known, and she saw all the excuses falling on me and she knew that I wanted to go see all that dancing and singing as opposed to getting my kick swinging on a trapeze. She approached my mother and said that I could go with her and that she would take good care of me. I instantly jumped at the idea and, after not too much resistance, I was told that I could attend.

The minstrel show came to town and they had a parade the afternoon before the big show that Saturday night. It was so wonderful, I couldn't wait.

That night Ellen came by and picked me up and we walked down to the fairground where the gigantic tent of F. W. Woolcott Minstrels had staked out as their performance area. We bought our tickets and were shown to a seating area. I went into the colored area with Ellen, but she said in a really sweet voice, "Honey, I'm afraid you are going to have to go over and sit with your white folks. But don't worry, I'll keep an eye on you. We'll wave to one another every so often."

I reluctantly got up from the colored section and went over to the white section which was pretty filled with people I didn't know. The show began and I had never seen so much enthusiasm and fun and jokes and music and dancing. I was sure that one way or the other I was going to get into this wonderland called show business. I can still close my eyes today and remember all the bright lights of the *F. W. Woolcott Minstrel Show.*

After the performance, Ellen was over in a flash to reclaim me from the white section. We talked animatedly on our way back home and she got a big kick out of how I said I was going to do something like that in my future. She laughed and delivered me into the hands of my mother who was waiting on our front porch for us. Ellen said she was afraid I was spoiled forever. My mother smiled and was glad that I had such a good time.

I never forgot that one magic night and how it did direct me into the world of fun and make believe which is the land of show business. I even used Ellen by name as one of the characters in my book *Contessa.*

Sorry I kind of got off track with my wishing you a belated birthday but such memories as the F. W. Woolcott MInstrels can last a lifetime.

Very best to one and all,
Love, Uncle Jack

LETTER 37

DARLENE

Dear Darlene,

Thank you so very much for the clever birthday greeting. I think it is very fun that someone used the sayings of Oscar Wild for greeting cards. I suspect you came upon these at the Los Angeles County gift shop. They have so many interesting things for sale. Oscar Wilde is one of my favorite writers and certainly inspired me to become a writer. I think my favorite saying of his is the one that goes, "No good deed ever goes unpunished." This particular saying reminds me of a good example which I would like to share with you since you are in the school teaching business.

Like so many stories, one has to begin at the very beginning for the tale to make much sense. Mine starts when I was a teacher of Spanish at New York State University in Plattsburg, New York. My position was a one-year contract and was not renewable because I did not have a PhD. I only had a master's degree even though it was from Middlebury College as well as The University of Madrid in Spain.

During the spring vacation of that year at the university Ken, my friend of eighteen years, and I went to Buenos Aires, Argentina during our spring break. It was only for a week, and we thought that would be enough time for us to check the place out. Check it out we did and found it to be one of the most delightful places we had ever been. In fact, we would like to have moved there. With that in mind I scouted around for teaching opportunities while I was there. I came upon a small private university called John F. Kennedy University. It of course was feeding off the theme of its patron saint, but it was a modern and very interesting place with great teachers and administrators.

I spoke with several people, including students, and found that the place was just fine, and they offered me a position as a teacher of English for the following year. That was wonderful. Ken would then be able to find some teaching position possibly with a private language school.

Here is where Oscar comes in. If I had just decided to move to Buenos Aires and taken the job, my life could've gone down a different trail. But no, my mind got off track. I rationalized that Buenos Aires was so far away and to uproot my life for the unknown life there, it would be quite an undertaking. I then decided that maybe I could do a good deed and I could kill two birds with one stone. I figured that if I could interest the powers that be in Plattsburg to have a group of our students from there go to JFK University for a Junior Year Abroad program that I could be the faculty advisor and would have a salary coming in while checking out Buenos Aires to see if I wanted to live there on a permanent basis.

The people at JFK were delighted and they certainly had a good faculty for such a proposition. They accepted my proposal. Now all I had to do was to go back to Plattsburg and, as a gesture of good will, would volunteer to shepherd the whole project. I made up some preliminary bulletins to pass out to students to see if indeed any such program would be of interest to our Plattsburg students. I was pleasantly surprised to find out that at least twenty-three or so were very interested. Then I had to write up a proposal for the project. The proposal had to be academic and pass the Dean's scrutiny. It also had to be approved by the University and if it got that far it would still have to be approved by the Governor's office in the capital of Albany. It was a monumental task and I had volunteered to do all the work.

There were people on the faculty and in the university system who loved the idea and some who hated it. A war broke out. Then twenty-three students made their wishes known that they wanted the opportunity. I found out that I would have to provide housing for twenty-three students. I had only just suggested the idea and now it was weighing on my back.

I was caught in the middle of an academic war while trying to keep the administrators at JFK in Buenos Aires on the hook. Terrible. It ended up that a compromise was made. Instead of Buenos Aires, the whole mess would take place at the university in Guadalajara, Mexico. By going to Guadalajara, the twenty-three students would engage in a tour of South America including Buenos Aires, Santiago, and other South American cities.

The full flower of Oscar's statement about no deed going unpunished started in full fashion just after our airplane took off from Miami headed to Quito, Ecuador. One of the twenty-three came up to me and said her toenail was hurting. I looked at it and the toenail did look sick. So, my first thing in Quito was to find a doctor who could take the toenail off. After that, there seemed to be a daily act of dipsomania on this tour. At one point, our bus was taking us to the airport to catch a flight to Rio. The hotel owner came running out with the police. It appears that one of my precious twenty-three had stolen everything in their hotel room that wasn't nailed down. So, they had to return all those ashtrays, towels, you name it and then we could be on our way. We finally did get to the University of Guadalajara and the powers that be in Albany cut the program to one semester instead of two. Ken and I found ourselves without employment in Guadalajara after that one semester. Yes, my good deed got well punished.

In the meantime, my very best to you and thanks again for the great card. It did stir up old memories, but it certainly taught me to watch out in the good deeds department.

Cheers,

Jack

LETTER 38

JANET-RUTHERFORD

Dear Ms. Janet Rutherford,

Thank you very much for the lovely birthday card. I appreciate the fact that you know me more than I realize because of your note in my birthday card. You mentioned you have read several of my plays, especially ones from *Paris Plays*. I was quite glad that you managed to reach me through the office of my former agent.

You wrote that you would like to know if a person like yourself, in their late fifties, could write a play or possibly begin writing. The answer is absolutely yes. The time to begin writing is when you start writing. There are a few tricks but nothing so complicated that you should feel that you need to join expensive workshops nor pay people to peruse your work for tips on how to improve it.

I can't exactly say that one can enter this profession without some help from a kind person or mentor. I know in my case; I was lucky enough to have a cousin who was a professional writer of short stories. She was my father's first cousin and her name was Sally Kelly.

When I first started trying to put my words on paper, I got up enough courage to have Sally take a look at it. Her reaction was to laugh. I was crushed. She told me that I had worlds to go but that I did have a spark. However, Sally went on to tell me that I should try again and again.

She asked me why I had tried a short story as the vehicle of my creation and imagination. I replied because she had written short stories that had been published in most of the popular magazines. She said that maybe short stories were not my cup of tea and said that perhaps I should try something else.

I must admit that even at this late stage in my writing career that I have never had a short story published. I wrote probably about a dozen or more during my late teens and even up into my early forties. Somehow, I thought at least one of them would click.

I decided that I would try my hand at writing a play. I had appeared in my junior and senior year high school plays and enjoyed the experiences but had not thought of ever writing a play. I took a look at the printed version of the play I had been in my senior year and thought I would follow it and write a play.

My play was a silly piece of high school fluff and the next year when I attended Mississippi State College I got together a group of people and we put on my play. I did not wait for someone to ask me to put on my play; I just put the play on myself. It had very good success.

I saw that play writing was my forte and I had a talent for dialogue and sociable plots.

Even though I wrote several plays after that, I did not have another of my plays performed until I lived in Paris, ten years later. During that time, I still tried my hand at short stories, thinking I could get someone to publish them. That simply did not happen and I finally gave up trying to write a short story and decided to write plays.

The first year I lived in Paris I took one of my short stories entitled *Killing Time* and turned it into a long one-act. The two characters consisted of a young girl and an old lady.

I rounded up some actors and I put the play on myself. This ultimately became The Paris English Theatre where eight of my plays were produced and those are the ones in the book of mine you read, an anthology of those eight plays called *Paris Plays*.

I put an ad in the Paris English language newspaper, *The International Herald Tribune*, for actors and also found a small café theater that would allow me to produce my play. The theater saw it as an opportunity to sell beer and peanuts and I saw it as my golden opportunity.

From the ad in the *Tribune*, lots of people showed up to read for the two parts in my play. My roommate Ken was in charge of casting and handling those who answered the ad. Ken would bring people into the small theater and they would read. Ken came in and said that the line outside was still kind of long. He said there was a young lady out there with some male friends and they were laughing and carrying on so maybe we should let the girl read and let them go their merry ways. The young lady had long straight hair and bangs and was kind of tall and thin. I talked with her briefly, asking her what she was doing in Paris. She said that she was studying modeling and pantomime. I told her in my estimation she should get rid of her bangs and cut her hair. I then had her read. She was okay but nervous. I thanked her and did not use her in my play.

About ten years later I was living in Los Angeles and was trying my hand at acting. I got a small job as an extra in the movie called *Frances*. The film starred the very talented and successful actress Jessica Lang.

The day arrived for my scene to be shot. I got into costume and makeup, went onto the set, and was told to wait for Miss Lange. She showed up and while we were chatting she asked me if I used to put on plays in Paris. I said yes and she said she had tried out for one of them and asked me if I remembered her and what advice I had given her. I didn't remember so she reminded me what I had said about her bangs and the long hair. I was thunderstruck to say the least. Then she grinned and said that she didn't get the part in my play. Obviously she had gone on to bigger and better things. We had a good time reminiscing about our times in Paris. After that I followed her career a bit and saw that she had gone on from *Francis* to other big films. I only bring this up because in this business you never know what will happen. You just try, try, and try.

So my advice to you, Janet, is to write that play and then get some actors together and see how it sounds and if your effort works. So, sure, you are never too old. Look at me. I'm eighty-nine and still writing.

Best to you and thanks again for the card.

Jack Fitzgerald

LETTER 39

SCOTT

Dear Scott,

Good to hear from you and thanks for remembering my birthday. It is hard to believe it was twenty years ago when we were neighbors in West Hollywood. You are still there but I moved here to Palm Springs in the late nineties. I still remember the good times we had in West Hollywood. I thought after I moved down here that I'd be back quite often in West Hollywood visiting such good friends as you. However, I guess the older we get the less we like to leave home. Anyway, it is great keeping in touch with you even if it is now down to just birthdays. You know you are welcome to visit here anytime you like.

In your card you mentioned that you often remember when we met in Guatemala and the adventures we had there. I too remember those times very well and I don't know if you remember but I wrote a play by the name of *Hotel Virginia* that was loosely based on our experiences there.

I was traveling down into southern Mexico to Guatemala and on to El Salvador with Joe, my schoolteacher friend. We made it okay from Southern California down through Mexico to the city of Oaxaca and visited the wonderful ruins there. We were to go from there on down to Guatemala but we heard from some fellow tourists that they had called off their trip to Guatemala because of so many terrorists. Joe and I were in a bit of a quandary about whether we should go on or turn back and go home. We both wanted so much to see the cities of Antigua and Chichicastenango and other beautiful places of interest. We decided we would continue on down to the Guatemalan border and check things out.

We had a good trip down. On our last night in Mexico we were having drinks and dinner at the hotel when we spotted you and your sister Sonya at a nearby table. You were speaking English so I started up a conversation. The four of us got to be good friends right away. We asked you what you had heard about conditions in Guatemala. You told us that you had heard there were active terrorists but that if we stayed on main roads we would probably be safe. Before the dinner was over the four of us had decided to travel together. We thought there was safety in numbers and we made that our motto as we continued on to see the beauty of Guatemala.

The next morning we drove to the border and cautiously crossed into Guatemala. The border authorities issued us stern warnings saying that we should be extra careful due to the terrorists. The four of us were quite willing to proceed but with a great deal of caution. Your sister Sonya was a real trooper and really fun to know.

One thing we agreed on was that Guatemala was one of the most colorful places we had ever visited. The countryside itself is beautiful with a manicured look. Nothing wild. Everything just gorgeous. The natives wore colorful clothing and it added to the beauty of the country.

For our first night we stayed in a hotel built on a coffee plantation. We agreed that Guatemalan coffee is just about the best we had ever tasted. Even today I bet you are still searching for it. Anyway, on that coffee plantation everything was just nice. As we had dinner together that first night, we marveled on how pretty everything was and how colorful. We laughed because the chickens were all white but had been dyed different colors. They certainly were a conversation starter.

The next day we headed to the native city of Chichicastenango which is inhabited mainly by people of Indian ancestry. Their clothes were super colorful and we visited it on market day. This was extremely fortunate because we got to see different tribes of people in one area. It was a wonderful place to shop and pick up all sorts of souvenirs. One of the beauty spots was the Church of Santo Tomás. Inside, the Indians prayed to the white man's god and then they would come outside to an alter and burn incense to their pagan gods. One thing the four of us agreed upon was that a camera could take perfect photos just by pointing it in any direction. I still have a beautiful photo I took of the church from outside with its incense altar.

We hated to leave after two days but headed toward Antigua. This colonial Spanish city had a beautiful cathedral as well as other splendid buildings. A nearby volcano erupted several hundred years ago and lava had covered the entire town. At the present, only the top of the church is visible, yet it is in perfect condition. The Spanish rebuilt the city and its cathedral. It is interesting to walk around the stone lava and inspect the steeple which did not get covered. This was a beautiful area and we were told that at a nearby lake was a small town well worth visiting if just for the day. We were enjoying things so much we could not turn down the temptation so on our way we went to the little town. We noticed that there was very little traffic and that kind of made us feel uneasy. Before we knew it some cars and trucks came from the bushy areas off the road and surrounded us. Yes, it was what we had dreaded, the terrorists. Sure enough they robbed us demanding all our money. They searched our cars and took what they thought was worth taking. They wanted to take Joe as a hostage. We argued with them not to take him, but they asked what we had to trade for him. Sonya took off a very nice ring she had as well as her high school class ring and said it was about all they had. Surely Joe was worth both rings. The school ring got their attention because it had meaning. Her other ring was just jewelry. So, Joe got delivered from the terrorists for one class ring. They allowed us to leave and we quickly made our way to the little town where we had intended to visit. We had no money and did not know what to do.

We saw that in the little town there were a couple of really nice hotels. We went to both of them but they could not help us because the terrorists had cut their telephone lines. They suggested we go to another hotel in town which was not very clean or nice, but the managers of the hotels said that he was sure the terrorists had left that hotels telephone lines intact.

We went to this hotel which was named *Hotel Virginia* and indeed it's telephone was working. We told the owner our plight and he said he would get in touch with the embassy in Guatemala City to come and get us. He was sure they would pay for our stay.

What we didn't realize until we moved in and were having dinner was that the place was a whore house. We nevertheless had a great time talking to the girls. One of them was named Chucha, a rather rotund lady who was quite fashionable in her own way. She obviously was the star prostitute of the place.

That night after dinner Chucha, in her broken English, sang songs to us and then told some Indian legends. It was a most unusual evening if you remember it as much as I do.

When it was time for bed, we found that the hotel rooms were not fit for us to stay in. We were told there were some native straw dwellings which were small but much better than our rooms. The owner said there was no bathroom in them. He said if we had to go to the bathroom at night to be careful because there were animals of the night afoot. That did not set well. You and your sister stayed together in one of the small cabins and Joe stayed in another and I stayed in a very small single. That night I had to go to the bathroom and ventured out go to the bathroom which was a bit of a distance. On returning to my cabin, I had the presence that someone or something was tracking me. I made it as quickly as I could to my cabin and locked the door behind me. Presently there was heavy breathing and something scratching on the door trying to get it. I could not imagine what it was but finally whatever it was went away. The next morning when I told the owner of my experience, he told me I was very lucky because a black panther had been sighted in the area. This did it. I was ready to return home.

And that we did once we got to Guatemala City, thanks to the owner of the *Hotel Virginia* and the American Embassy people. All in all, it was an exciting trip and one I am glad we shared. Meeting you and your sister was a real treat.

Years later, in my Paris English Theatre, I wrote a play called *Hotel Virginia* and it starred Chucha and sundry events connected with our stay in that little town. I don't know if you have a copy of my book *Paris Plays* but my play *Hotel Virginia* is there.

My very best to you, Scott. Tell Sonja I said hi.

Cheers, your buddy,
Jack

LETTER 40

CHARLOTTE

Dear Charlotte,

Thanks for your very welcomed birthday card. I must say that I look forward to your family photo greeting card that you send out yearly. See what I get for introducing you to my friend Richard so many years ago? I do miss Richard now that he is no longer with us. His spirit lives on though. I have kept all of your photo Christmas cards and have watched as you had your first two children and then their children who are pretty much grown by now.

I know the last time we talked on the phone you were asking me questions about how I ended up living in Paris for ten years. I intended getting back to on this but like many things in life we put them off and they never get done. So, I will take this moment to correct that fault of mine and answer you fully. You and Richard were always so supportive of my exploits and it is only fair that I let you in on details.

To begin with, you knew my friend Ken. He was a roommate and traveling companion. You two even came to visit us several times in Pairs when we lived there. But that is getting ahead of the story.

My living in France for ten years began in Guadalajara, Mexico. I was teaching Spanish at New York State University in Plattsburg and in charge of a group of students living abroad. Originally, I was to take the group to Buenos Aires but that got cut to Guadalajara instead. It was supposed to be for a year but it ended up being cut to a single semester.

In September of that year, twenty-three students, Ken, and I set off for our trip. The semester went by and it was truly a daunting task shepherding twenty-three students, each one with special needs and problems. It turned out to be quite a complicated task. The semester ended in December and Ken and I, as well as the twenty-three students, were slated to return to Plattsburg. This city is in upper state New York and winter is spelled with a capital W there. Winters are tough. Guadalajara was sunny and bright but there was no way we could stay there.

Ken and I got three days off to get back to Plattsburg and face all that winter. We had already decided that Plattsburg was only going to last until the end of that school year for both of us due to the extreme winters. We were in a quandary of what to do. Ken, who had always wanted to live in Paris, France, suggested that we both take off the semester and instead of returning Plattsburg, we would go to Paris. I discovered that Air Bahama, a division of Icelandic Airlines, flew from the Bahamas to Luxembourg and had a very wonderful price for a forty-five-day maximum stay. Ken and I thought that this would be the answer. We did manage to get the winter semester off in Plattsburg. We flew from Guadalajara to Miami, then to the Bahamas, and from there to Luxembourg, and then by train to Paris.

We arrived in Paris with no place to go and no idea of what would be coming next in our lives. We took the Metro from the airport to Place de la Opera. We walked up those steps which empty out into a glorious sight. The golden dome of the Charles Garnier Paris Opera and the fabled and fabulous Place de la Opera. With our suitcases in hand, we stared at that incredible sight and wondered what was next.

We stayed in a nearby small hotel for a couple days while we found a place on the rue de Cambon, near Chanel and the Ritz Hotel, where we could rent a room by the week or month. We were not flush with money, so we had to be very careful because Paris is not an inexpensive city.

Ken was in heaven. He had always dreamed of living in Paris. I loved it too but he could speak French while I spoke none. The second day Ken was there he scouted around and found a nearby private English Language school. He was offered a couple of classes and began teaching. I enrolled in the Alliance Francais to study French.

Our time went by fast, fast, fast. Ken did not want to leave Paris. He wanted to give up everything back in the states and live in Paris. I was slated to return to Plattsburg though without Ken. I could not see myself staying in Paris as I had no income and I didn't really speak all that much French in spite of my lessons at the Alliance.

Ken definitely decided to forfeit his airline ticket and remain in Paris. I had no other choice except to go back to Plattsburg and take up my job teaching Spanish there. Several days before we had this talk, the director of the school where Ken taught asked if I could fill-in for one of their teachers who had to return to the states. It amounted to almost a full-time job. Ken rationalized that with both of us working, we could make Paris work. I was between a rock and a hard place. At the last day of my airline ticket's validation, I decided to throw caution to the wind and stay in Paris with Ken.

So, Charlotte, that resulted in my living in Paris.

I remained in Paris for ten years. During that time, I became director of a language school, founded the Paris English Theatre, and fully launched myself into a writing career.

Ken remained at his school for several years and later became the director of a large language school until he retired. He has now been living in Paris for nearly fifty years. He partnered with a very interesting French person in the world of book publishing.

There you have it. Sometimes fate does make our decisions for us and Paris was an example of that. I would never have thought that I would end up in that city. Ken got his dream and is still living there and enjoying every day.

My best to you and your family, Charlotte.

Cheers,
Jack

LETTER 41

BRIAN

Dear Brian,

Thanks so much for the birthday card. My turning eighty-nine years old has made me reflect on so much that has happened in my life. I think the most adventuresome set of circumstances would have to be the around-the-world trip you, Ken, Richard, Steve, and I took in 1967. Would you agree?

It all began after seeing the film *Around the World Eighty Days*. It made me want to do the same thing. I could only imagine how exciting it would be to actually go around the world. The next thing I knew was my beginning to check out how one would go about such a venture. I went to a local travel agency to check out the possibilities of doing something as wild as this.

I met with Carol and she turned out to be a kind person who could see how much adventure I had in my soul. She said that she could work up such a trip via Pan Am Airways, long since gone out of business, which was the major airline of its time and went just everywhere. I left her office with the seed planted in my brain that, yes, I wanted to do such a trip. I knew I could not do this by myself. It did not take me long to convince my roommate, Ken, of such a proposition. The first question he asked was where is the money coming from to do such a trip. I told him I had not even gotten that far yet but now that we were there let's talk it about. I told Ken that I would have to borrow the money from the teacher's credit union by calling the trip educational. Ken said that he was sure he could ask his grandmother for most or part of the money.

With the idea firmly planted in my brain, I went back to see Carol and timidly asked her if she had any idea how much it would cost to go around the world. She was pleased that I had made it to the first base in my dream. She told me that it would take over a week to research it and come up with a tentative trip plan and price. I told her everything had to be done on the cheap.

A week later Carol contacted me and asked me to come see her at her office. I went and took Ken with me. She, without any formality, told us our trip was possible, but the price would be $2,200. At that time that sounded like a fortune. It really sounded impossible. She looked at me and asked if there was any way we could afford that. She said that to get this special price there would be a minimum of five or six people going on the trip. This meant we had to get three more people.

It was lucky, Brian, that I ran into you at your grandmother's birthday party where she said she would help if you wanted to go. You then pitched the dream to Richard, a fellow teacher at our school. I had a good friend at my school named Steve and I talked him into the dream. After a lot of meeting and talking, we got the five around-the-world travelers lined up.

We decided we would leave on the last day of school in June and return the first of September for the opening of school. With a bit of help from our principals at our schools, we did fit our time frame into eighty days.

We spent months figuring out things. As you well remember, since I came up with the idea, I pretty much was our chief in this adventure. Carol arranged a wonderful trip for us, and it did take in eighty days. It took a lot of planning and a lot of finagling to come up with the money for the trip as well as some spending money.

We took off the first of June. We flew from Los Angeles to Lima, Peru. When we arrived in Lima, we were dressed in coats and ties and looked more like missionaries than tourists. We arrived well-dressed but our suitcases did not.

We had packed very carefully to have just the bare minimum to get by for eighty days. So, what were we to do? We went ahead to our rendezvous in Iquitos, Peru. The main attraction there is the Eiffel House, built by the same Eiffel who built the tower in Paris. We got into a boat there to go down to a native area. We could hardly believe we were in the jungles of the Amazon. The natives we visited wore grass skirts, painted themselves red and, with blow guns, felled monkeys from the trees. Their big diet and spread for visiting tourists was monkey meat. The monkeys were put in a big pot and boiled. Then the people of the tribe would stand about the big pot and pull off meat and eat it. As fate would have it, the monsoon hit and we were instantly flooded and couldn't get out of this tributary back onto the Amazon for our return trip to Iquitos. We were wearing the same clothes we had left Los Angeles in and we were sweaty and feeling awful. Ken tried the boiled monkey and commented the usual, "It tastes like chicken."

We did finally get out of the place even though we were behind in our travel schedule. We made it back to Lima where the airline had found our suitcases which had mistakenly been sent to Germany. We then went to Rio in Brazil and attended Samba school, a dancing, marching, and drumming club to prepare to parade during Carnival. From Rio we took off for Madrid but had to turn around due to mechanical problems and took another flight later. This too caused a bit of delay.

We finally got to Madrid and from there went to Paris, Berlin, Munich, Vienna, Rome, and Italy, where we had a great time playing tourists. From Rome we flew to Israel. They had just had the Six-Day war. We had visas to go on to Egypt but, due to the war, we could not go.

We had many adventures. We were in the tail-end of the six-day war in Israel, an earthquake in Turkey, the snake temple in Penang, Malaysia, where snakes come back to stay for the season in this shrine. If you like snakes, this was the place. From there we went to Pakistan where they were in a conflict with India. We walked across no man's land in the fighting area to get to India. From there on to Hong Kong, Thailand, Japan and then back to Los Angeles.

Yes, the world is round, as we found out. Unfortunately, due to all the slow downs, wars, and natural disasters we were late for the opening of school. Our trip took eighty-seven days instead of eighty.

So many memories. Think of the pictures we took and the many showings of them to others after the trip. As the five of us said, it proves if you get an idea to do something, it will happen if you put your mind to it. In our case, it did happen. So now you and I as well as our traveling companions can safely say we had a world of fun.

Best to you, as always,
Jack

Kabul, Afghanistan, 1968.

Amazon natives, 1968.

Destroyed tank outside Tel Aviv from Israeli 6 Day War, 1968.

LETTER 42

MELISSA

Dear Melissa,

I was so glad to hear from you. It has been quite a spell with lots of water under the bridge. However, it was great hearing from you and I thank you for the birthday card. In your card you mentioned the grit and determination it took to put on the play you recently saw of mine, *The Apollo Experiment*.

I must admit that the two words grit and determination are words that remind me of my father. He did live long enough to see one of my plays, *Good Grief*, which I wrote when I was eighteen years old. Talk about grit and determination, it took a lot to put on that play but the one you saw was performed at the American Church in Paris some years back for sure. It took more grit and determination as *Good Grief* at Mississippi State College.

My father was an orphan. Both of his parents died before he was two years old. An aunt took him in to live with her. She had very few resources to sustain herself. She had lost her husband in an accident during the first year of their marriage. She existed mainly by selling butter, cheese, milk, and cakes. In her financial situation she still took in her deceased sister's youngest two children, my father Everett, and his sister, Nanny Lou. They lived on a farm in Egypt, Mississippi. When my father was six years old he was the major salesman for her products in their community. He worked so diligently that he earned the nickname Grits for his determination to help his aunt in her financial situation. He went to school but his entrepreneurial activities consumed most of his time. This kept up until he was twelve. By that time his aunt, sister, and he had moved from Egypt to Okolona. The one thing that made Okolona seem like a metropolis was the Gulf, Mobile, and the Ohio Railroad which ran through the city and was a hub for other smaller rail links.

Everett, or Grits, saw that his future was linked with Ohio Railroad. He gave up working at a local mill and began working for the railroad as a means of keeping himself and his aunt and sister alive. He became a "Hey Boy." This means he worked the passenger waiting room and would go get people drinks and sandwiches for tips. He then added some candy bars and bottled drinks to his inventory. This he did with success due to his enthusiasm, grit, and determination. He still tried to go to school when he could. When he was twelve, he gave up school and never graduated from high school.

His grit and determination were noticed and, at the age of eighteen, he was offered a regular job with the railroad. This upgraded the living conditions of his aunt, sister, and himself.

With grit and determination, he taught himself Greek, Latin, and Spanish. He instilled these values in his two sons and adopted daughter.

So, Melissa, your card hit the spot for me in remembering how important in life grit and determination are. Thanks so much for getting into contact. I do hope we write one another more often.

Thanks again, with affection,
Jack

Aunt Ripple, my father, and my mother, 1970.

Printed in the United States
by Baker & Taylor Publisher Services